With My Prayers,
Carole "Lisa Lynn" Gilbert
Matthew 6:33

Unraveled,
TIME TO HEAR

An Investment Toward Your Eternity

LISA LYNN

WESTBOW
PRESS®
A DIVISION OF THOMAS NELSON
& ZONDERVAN

WestBow Press books may be ordered through booksellers or by contacting:

WestBow Press
A Division of Thomas Nelson & Zondervan
1663 Liberty Drive
Bloomington, IN 47403
www.westbowpress.com
1 (866) 928-1240

ISBN: 978-1-9736-4216-9 (sc)
ISBN: 978-1-9736-4217-6 (hc)
ISBN: 978-1-9736-4215-2 (e)

Library of Congress Control Number: 2018912083

Print information available on the last page.

WestBow Press rev. date: 10/12/2018

From the author of the autobiography, *Unraveled, Time to Tell*

To you, the reader, I wish you this prayer:

> God, my God, hear my prayer. Be with me, guide me, and forgive me. I'm a person unworthy of Your love. I hurt the ones I love the most and cater to the ones I love the least. I want to be Yours! I believe Jesus is Your Son, who came to this earth and died on a shameful cross, but made that a cross a day of victory and eternal blessing for me and any who gives his life to you for You. Thank You, Jesus! Thank You, God! And thank You for the gift of Your Spirit! Amen!

If you prayed this in your heart, you are now prepared to experience a deeper knowledge of God, Jesus, and the Holy Spirit. You have also prepared your heart for a deeper understanding of sin and a deeper guidance through prayer.

Contents

Introduction

Do you ever need guidance and understanding in grasping your everyday situations? When life is hard, the need arouses for guidance, specifically of a supernatural kind. We need to realize we're not searching for answers but seeking the answer that is already there.

Unraveled, Time to Hear gives us the knowledge and guidance from this supernatural one with the answers we seek. It takes faith—our faith—to a deeper understanding. Also included in this book are questions with room to answer for your own eye-opening, heart-awakening conclusions. It is a freestanding guide but correlates with my autobiography, *Unraveled, Time to Tell,* which gives insight into my learned knowledge from God about each subject in this book.

You do not have to read *Unraveled, Time to Tell* (UTTT) first to understand this book. Chapters from UTTT will be listed at the end in case you do want to further your knowledge of God's Word in the hard situations that we go through. You can reference my autobiography or use it as a backup tool if you want or even use it later.

So much of these sections in *Unraveled, Time to Hear* will be subjects you already know or have already heard. It will test you in your knowledge of God and His Word. It is meant to review and refresh as well as to learn and apply.

Why test our knowledge? If we, as believers, already know the correct behaviors, then why aren't we acting as believers? And if you think we are, look at our world, its crises, and its views. This guide, if used as a study, can be completed in up to three months depending on how many chapters you want to do in a week. You may also read it on your own at your own pace. It includes questions to contemplate and answer and may be discussed within a group.

"Fight the good fight of faith; take hold of the eternal life to which you were called" (1 Timothy 6:12 NASB). "But seek ye first the kingdom of God, and His righteousness; and all these things shall be added unto you" (Matthew 6:33 KJV).

You may ask, "From where do you get your authority to write this book? Who are you to write this? What is your credibility?"

My authority, credibility, knowledge, and guidance come from God, along with His Word, my belief in Jesus in my heart, and the Holy Spirit interceding for me with the words given. It may be hard to understand how someone could receive great joy and blessing from sharing about great tragedy and hardship. Our God is amazing, and through Him I do this:

> And the Spirit said to Philip, "Go over and join this chariot." So Philip ran to him and heard him reading Isaiah the prophet and asked, "Do you understand what you are reading?" And he said, "How can I, unless someone guides me?" And he invited Philip to come up and sit with him. Now the passage of the Scripture that he was reading was this: "Like a sheep he was led to the slaughter and like a lamb before its shearer is silent, so he opens not his mouth. In his humiliation justice was denied him. Who can describe his generation? For his life is taken away from the earth." And the eunuch said to Philip, "About whom, I ask you, does the prophet say this, about himself or someone else?" Then Philip opened his mouth, and beginning with this Scripture he told him the good news about Jesus. (Acts 8:29–35 ESV)

We also, like Philip, are to tell the good news about Jesus. I have over fifty years of learning God's Word by living it and living against it. My experiences far outweigh any knowledge I could get from any other books than the Bible, although I have read and studied plenty, and I'm still learning and always hoping to be. I do believe other books are great aids in our knowledge if we carefully screen the authors.

And just like the books, my main teacher is far greater than any professor with any amount of degrees, but these professors are also great aids in furthering our knowledge and understanding if we carefully make sure they are following God's Word. God calls some to be teachers, like Himself, but He also calls some to be like Philip. Philip didn't have the teaching like the Bible scholars of those days, but he had firsthand knowledge of Christ, our Lord. In my writing, I rely on my God—my heavenly Father, my Yahweh, my El Shaddai—as my teacher and guide.

As you read this, keep in mind that everything you read in this book is how I've concluded it to be. There are some questions this side of heaven that are simply unanswerable, and some inquiries we put emphasis on aren't important enough to spend time trying to answer anyway.

I believe this book gives the most important aspects a believer of Jesus Christ is to follow, to learn, to use, and to teach using all scripture together. All its applications are, as is said, tried and true.

"All Scripture is breathed out by God and profitable for teaching, for reproof, for correction, and for training in righteousness, that the man of God may be complete, equipped for every good work" (2 Timothy 3:16-17 ESV).

Also all answers we think we have today are subject to change as God reveals Himself to us more and more as we mature and learn and use His Word.

"Let the word of Christ dwell in you richly, teaching and admonishing one another in all wisdom, singing psalms and hymns and spiritual songs, with thankfulness in your hearts to God. And whatever you do, in word or deed, do everything in the name of the Lord Jesus, giving thanks to God the Father through him" (Colossians 3:16–17 ESV).

And never stop singing. The heart can dry up.

I stand straight and tall
That my light may never dim,
All for Him.

I fill my cup with faith
To the brim,
All for Him.

I laugh and run for joy,
As on a whim,
All for Him.

I give my life and hang
On the farthest limb,
All for Him.

Introduction to Section 1

The Trinity

Our God, His Son Jesus, and the Holy Spirit

God's Word is accurate and true in all it affirms. We are not to read the stories and think our sin is okay, but rather read them as examples of what not to do. We are forgiven, but we are not always given approval. Our actions do have consequences and repercussions, not to mention the way our actions affect others.

An example of this would be David and Bathsheba. It is not okay to have infidelity. But from God's Word, we learn how God views that. All scripture is inspired by God and true to His commands for our lives.

I'm afraid a lot of people believe the Bible and God is real but don't believe His commands pertain to them. It's like believing a historical event is actual and true but at the same time not believing it has any significance directly to their life.

If an event were important enough to be recorded historically, it has important significance to our lives directly somehow. It has molded or changed our laws, our economics, and every aspect of our lives. The same is true for God, Jesus, the Holy Spirit, and every word in the Bible, only so much more. It actually is so much more. It means life or death to every person!

"Show me the path where I should go, O Lord; point out the right road for me to walk. Lead me; teach me; for you are the God who gives me salvation. I have no hope except in you" (Psalm 25:4–5 LB).

Now let's look at and open up our thoughts. Don't be afraid. You don't have to have big church words. This is for your and God's eyes only.

Who is God?

_____

_____

_____

_____

_____

_____

_____

_____

_____

Who is Jesus?

_____

_____

_____

_____

_____

_____

_____

_____

_____

_____

Who is the Holy Spirit?

_____

_____

_____

_____

_____

_____

_____

_____

_____

_____

Who is the Trinity? How do you explain the Trinity to yourself?

_____

_____

_____

_____

_____

_____

_____

_____

_____

These questions will be discussed in detail from God's Word and by His guidance. The Trinity is as hard to understand as it is to explain. It is in reference to God the Father, Jesus the Son, and the Holy Spirit, God's spirit. The Trinity is the "three head," the alpha and omega, the beginning and the end.

Peter explains the Trinity to us in such a simple way, "Dear friends, God the Father chose you long ago and knew you would become His children. And the Holy Spirit has been at work in your hearts, cleansing You with the blood of Jesus Christ and making you to please him" (1 Peter 1:2 LB).

You will learn how these three are separate, but at the same time, they are the same. You will learn how they perform specific roles but together work the wonderful completion in us, all for their glory.

Our God will and has given us the knowledge to understand and know how to live our lives knowing Him and in a way pleasing to

Him. We have to understand the power of our heavenly Father, the peace, patience, and provision that only comes from Him. We need to know how to rely on Him! Do I always do this? No! I fall short also. But as we learn about the Trinity, we start to understand their place in all sovereignty, and we start relying on them more each day. We have to learn to be able to do this. Let's get started.

Chapter 1

Our God

"Then Moses said to God, 'Behold, I am going to the sons of Israel, and I shall say to them, 'The God of your fathers has sent me to you.' Now they may say to me, 'What is his name?' What shall I say to them?' And God said to Moses, 'I AM WHO I AM'; and He said, 'Thus you shall say to the sons of Israel, 'I AM has sent me to you'" (Exodus 3:13–14 NASB).

God is very specific but gives us a large number of names to call Him. These names are in His Word, the Bible, and in the different languages of those who worshipped Him. Here are some of my favorites:

- Jehovah (Lord)
- Jehovah-Raah (the Lord My Shepherd)
- Jehovah Rapha (the Lord That Heals)
- Jehovah Shammah (the Lord Is There)
- Jehovah Mekoddishkem (the Lord Who Sanctifies You)
- Elohim (the Creator)
- El Shaddai (the All-Sufficient One)
- Adonai (Lord, Master)
- Yahweh (Lord, Jehovah)
- El Olam (the Everlasting God)

I love what *Smith's Bible Dictionary* says.

> The meaning of Jehovah is *underived existence*, HE IS, or I AM BECAUSE I AM, the God of Abraham, of grace, and truth, and love; self-existence, eternity. Elohim is God *in nature*, Jehovah is God *in grace*. The word Jehovah is supposed to mean YAHU, *joy*; VAH, *pain*-the God of good and evil.

Why is it important to know God's names and the ones He gives Himself? We need to know how to worship and revere Him as well as realize just how big He really is and just how big He really is to us. We need to understand His immeasurableness yet reachability. In Old Testament times, names showed character and personality. I believe this is one reason God has so many names: His character and traits are never ending. "Let them praise the name of the Lord, for His name alone is exalted; His glory is above earth and heaven" (Psalm 148:13 NASB).

What name do you use for God? Do you use Father, heavenly Father, Lord, or some other name? Did you call Him a certain name in your remarks at the beginning of this session?

Now let's look at some other verses about God and His greatness. I will be using the King James Version on some of these. Some important words have been changed in translations over the years, losing some of their emphasis.

> Fill their faces with shame; that they may seek thy name, O Lord. Let them be confounded and troubled forever; yea, let them be put to shame, and perish: That men may know that thou, whose name alone is Jehovah, art the most high over all the earth. (Psalm 83:16–18 KJV)

Here our Lord's name is called Jehovah. This name puts more personable emphasis on the greatness of God and gives more profoundness to the prayer, don't you agree? In newer translations, the name Jehovah has been changed to Lord, as can be seen when comparing the King James and English Standard Versions.

- "The secret of the Lord is with them that fear him; and he will shew them his covenant" (Psalm 25:14 KJV).
- "The friendship of the Lord is for those who fear him, and he makes known to them his covenant" (Psalm 25:14 ESV).

God Himself urges us to have a close relationship with Him. That's one reason to know His names! "For the eyes of the Lord move to and fro throughout the earth that He may strongly support those whose heart is completely His. You have acted foolishly in this. Indeed, from now on you will surely have wars" (2 Chronicles 16:9 NASB).

Jehovah will use His power however He wants for those who love Him. And He is watching and evaluating us and our actions. "God is gracious and loving. He is just and wrathful" (Psalms 17, 89, 145; 1 John 4:8).

> The Lord is righteous in all his ways, and holy in all his works. The Lord is nigh unto all them that call upon him, to all that call upon him in truth. He will fulfil the desire of them that fear him: he also will hear their cry, and will save them. The Lord preserveth all them that love him: but all the wicked will he destroy. (Psalm 145:17–20 KJV)

Definitions

- Nigh: near
- Fear: revere; respect; awe

From the day we were born, we thought of nothing but ourselves. We desired only for ourselves. We lived only to please ourselves (Psalm 51:5). But that wasn't to remain (Psalm 51:14). There was, is, and always will be a higher being. That is our God! "He performs wonders that cannot be fathomed, miracles that cannot be counted" (Job 9:10 NIV).

Here we see Job in all his misery, despair, and discouragement, even from God, and yet Job still recognizes God's greatness. He was there witnessing God firsthand, even without seeing Him.

I can tell you about my mother firsthand. She's been gone almost fifty years as I write this, but I remember where she worked, her hobbies, our trip to the circus on the bus, Christmas, the times she had to spank me, and so much more because I was there. I was with her then and later when she wasn't with me in person.

I could remember how wonderful and special she made me feel. That's what Job is doing here. He was there with God. He knew things about God. And even when God was silent, Job knew God was there and how He felt. He writes the verse above when he was at a heightened feeling of hopelessness. Later we read of Job's understanding of the outcome of God's tests. Job knows he will "come out as gold" (Job 23:8–12). And we know Job never faltered in his love and faithfulness toward God.

What does this have to do with my mom? I went through all these same emotions toward my mom for dying, and I even felt the same way toward God for allowing it. But I can look back now and see that, even when I wasn't listening and obeying and even when I was blaming God, I still knew Him and His greatness.

And He was there! Like Job, I understand the outcome, which now includes sharing with you what God shared with me (2 Corinthians 1:3–5). And like Job's story, my story has an ending that will be happy for eternity. "O Lord, open my lips, and my mouth will declare your praise" (Psalm 51:15 ESV).

I heard a quote on the radio that sums up the difference between humans and God. A preacher named Tony Evans said, "If we had the power of God, we'd change everything. If we had the wisdom of God, we'd change nothing." This same preacher also said, "The absence of unity is the absence of God. When God sees unity, He will bless."

In 1 Corinthians 1:10, Paul urges the church to be unified "in the same mind and same judgement." If we had God's wisdom, we'd be unified. Then we'd see God's healing and His blessings, and we wouldn't feel the need for change. We are the church, His people. And God's will is to be done. We are to make His name known to others and help in furthering His kingdom for His glory. This is our life's purpose. Knowing this frees us to understand and give instead of expecting to receive.

Definitions

- Church: the Lord's faithful people, us
- Kingdom of God (kingdom of heaven): God's rule on the earth and His kingdom to come when Jesus returns

"Thy kingdom come. Thy will be done in earth, as it is in heaven" (Matthew 6:10 KJV). "For I am the Lord, I change not; therefore ye sons of Jacob are not consumed" (Malachi 3:6 KJV).

Malachi is the last book of the Old Testament, and it is the last of the prophetic books giving us insight into what is to come. We see in this verse that what is to come is actually what has always been. God's purpose hasn't changed and won't because He hasn't changed and won't.

Therefore, what God meant for the sons of Israel and Jacob could not change, even if they didn't always follow God. What reassurance for us! What God has planned for the end, He began at the beginning. And it includes and will be not changed for us, as believers.

This is our almighty God, and this is His promise! "Therefore we do not lose heart. Though outwardly we are wasting away, yet inwardly we are being renewed day by day. For our light and momentary troubles are achieving for us an eternal glory that far outweighs them all" (2 Corinthians 4:16–17 NIV).

What are your thoughts of God now?

_____

_____

_____

_____

_____

_____

_____

_____

_____

_____

Are they any different?

_____

_____

_____

_____

_____

_____

_____

_____

_____

"So, whether you eat or drink, or whatever you do, do all to the glory of God" (1 Corinthians 10:31 ESV). "Oh, taste and see that the LORD is good! Blessed is the man who takes refuge in him!" (Psalm 34:8 ESV).

Chapter 2

Jesus

G od said to Moses in the Old Testament, "I Am who I Am," and He instructs Moses to tell the people of Israel, "I Am has sent me to you." In the New Testament, Thomas, a disciple of Jesus, asks Jesus a question. Jesus answered, "I am the way and the truth and the life. No one comes to the Father except through me" (John 14:6 NIV).

The Old and New Testaments tell with certainty who God and Jesus are. David Platt, pastor and author, says, "Who you say Jesus is will determine everything about how you follow Him." We need to check ourselves. Do you know how you follow Jesus?

Jesus shed His blood on the cross for the salvation of our sins. If that sounds cliché, then that's a cliché to say. And we need to say it over and over and over to refresh our memories and remind ourselves and to pass it on.

My brother was accused of the horrible crime of shooting our mother. After he was released from juvenile detention, we would spend as much time together as possible, like we did before the crime occurred.

One afternoon we were running in the woods behind our grandparents' house, looking for old bottles, as we had done years before. My brother had his BB gun, which was a normal thing to have in the woods.

As we were running, he abruptly turned, and when he did, it

startled me since I was following right behind him. I never had any thought other than the normal startled reaction anyone would have.

But confused by my movement, he looked at me and exclaimed, "You too?"

I knew what he was referring too. He thought I blamed him as well. The look on his face broke my heart! I say all this to help us feel what Jesus felt. If we could imagine the look on His face as He hung on the cross looking down on mankind, knowing some didn't understand, so many didn't believe, and that this would continue throughout history. Do you think His thoughts might've included "You too?"

No, Jesus's thoughts were "You too!" He knew He came to this earth for our salvation, and He knew that's why He was demonstrating the ultimate sacrifice to us. We were all included in His thoughts as He hung on that cross that day. It is for us to believe! You too?

"Because of the miracles he did in Jerusalem at the Passover celebration, many people were convinced that he was indeed the Messiah. But Jesus didn't trust them, for he knew mankind to the core. No one needed to tell him how changeable human nature is!" (John 2:23–25 LB). Jesus was accused of a horrible crime, an act He was not guilty of! Do we believe or blame Him today?

Let's look at the specific things we know about Jesus:

- He was born of a virgin (Matthew 1:23; Isaiah 7:14).
- The angel Gabriel told his mother Mary of this miraculous event (Luke 1).
- Jesus was all about good news, from His birth and life being prophesied in the Old Testament (Isaiah 7:14, 9:6, 11:1–5, 53; Daniel 7:13–14; Zechariah 13:1, to name a few) all the way to His birth, teachings, death, and second coming in the New Testament.

Everything—His whole life, whole death and resurrection, message, and meaning—is good news!

So why was His life so filled with sorrow and all things that seemed wrong? It wasn't and isn't Jesus, but mankind—which was and still is sinful and wrong—leaves sadness in so many situations. After all, this is why God sent Him, His only Son, whom He loved, to die for mankind and save us (mankind) from our sins and wrongfulness. And to those of us who believe, commit, and follow Jesus, we are freed and cleansed from our sin and wrongful ways. Jesus is not a fictional story of those biblical times, but a real joyful, living hope. He is not sorrow and pain, but joy, peace, and love. And He rejoices in heaven with God for us.

"Then he was filled with the joy of the Holy Spirit and said, "I praise you, O Father, Lord of heaven and earth, for hiding these things from the intellectuals and worldly wise and for revealing them to those who are as trusting as little children. Yes, thank you, Father, for that is the way you wanted it" (Luke 10:21 LB). Notice that not only Jesus and God but the Holy Spirit also, the Trinity, is rejoicing for us! Wow, what a thought!

Jesus grew up with a normal family although He was never normal. His father on earth was a carpenter. We know Jesus went to the temple to study His heavenly Father's Word, mostly from the book of Isaiah, as a young boy. Later in His life, Jesus quotes Isaiah in many situations.

Jesus knew why He was sent to earth from His heavenly throne. "For I came down from heaven, not to do mine own will, but the will of Him that sent me" (John 6:38 KJV).

And Jesus knew what His job and purpose were. "So everyone who acknowledges me before men, I also will acknowledge before my Father who is in heaven" (Matthew 10:32 RSV). "For this is my blood of the new testament, which is shed for many for the remission of sins" (Matthew 26:28 KJV).

This is how we have a relationship with God, through Jesus Christ, His Son. This is why Jesus came, to save us from our sins and a destructive lifestyle. The psalmist understood who to cry out to for salvation from their enemies, as we read in Psalm 118:25 and from David in Psalm 3. The crowd in Jerusalem knew this, as we know from Matthew 21:9. They were shouting to "Hosanna," which means "save us." They knew who Jesus was and why He came.

And yet Jesus had the same emotions as us, and in several

instances, we can read of His turning to God Himself for guidance. We also can read of His moment of asking God to change His ultimate job, His "cup," if it were God's will (Matthew 26:39; Mark 14:35–36; Luke 22:42).

Jesus was determined and evidenced to fulfill what He was here to do for us. And He was elevated by His heavenly Father God for completing His purpose, His "cup!" He was God, and He was human (Hebrews 2:17–18).

I've always loved the example used about your cup being "half full" versus being "half empty." That is, it's how positive people see the cup one way and negative people see the cup another when, in reality, the cup is at the same level. I've always thought of my cup as half full because I am a positive-minded person, but I did go through a period of years where the negativity took over, mostly because of sinfulness. During that time, I felt my cup was half empty. We should all realize— when we have Jesus on our side and in our hearts and when we truly know Him, who He is, and what He did for us—our cup is not only full but overflowing. Where do you see the level in your cup?

John wrote of Jesus and God, "There is no fear in love, but perfect love casts out fear. For fear has to do with punishment, and whoever fears has not been perfected in love. We love because he first loved us" (1 John 4:18–19 ESV).

There Jesus was, saving us (mankind), an ungrateful people. He came for all if only we believe. But we don't want to go that deep— that emotional—toward Jesus. We only want the good, righteous, cleansing, pure tangibles He has to offer. I find it ironic that He hung there covered in pain, injury, and blood, looking down on us (mankind) when, before He entered this world, He was looking down on us (mankind), covered in righteousness, pureness, and glory Himself, the very things we want from Him.

Jesus came to give us lifesaving salvation, eternity with Him in heaven, and peace while on this earth knowing this. And sometimes we have to suffer just like Jesus did. For it has been granted to you on behalf of Christ not only to believe in him but also to suffer for him (Philippians 1:29 NIV).

Jesus was laid in the tomb, but He did not stay there. As prophesied, three days later, He appeared to Mary Magdalene early on the first day of the week.

> On the evening of that day, the first day of the week, the doors being locked where the disciples were for fear of the Jews, Jesus came and stood among them and said to them, "Peace be with you." When he had said this, he showed them his hands and his side. Then the disciples were glad when they saw the Lord. Jesus said to them again, "Peace be with you. As the Father has sent me, even so I am sending you." (John 20:19–21 ESV)

Wow! I could almost stop this whole book on those verses alone, but I won't. Jesus gives us everything with His peace, but unfortunately we want this peace to mean we have everything we want the way we want and when we want it.

That's not what peace even is. Peace means to have harmony or freedom from strife or dissension. It is a state of tranquility. If you live in worldly ways, you are never free from strife or dissension. You will never have harmony, and you will never know tranquility because you know that's not what God has meant for your life. Philippians 1:27–29, of which we read verse 29 above, tells us suffering and faith go together and are from God. Both are equally privileges given to us through Jesus.

What are your thoughts of Jesus now?

_____

_____

_____

_____

_____

_____

_____

_____

_____

_____

Are they any different?

_____

_____

_____

_____

_____

_____

_____

_____

_____

_____

"For God so loved the world, that he gave his only Son, that whoever believes in him should not perish but have eternal life. For God did not send his Son into the world to condemn the world, but in order that the world might be saved through him" (John 3:16–17 ESV).

Chapter 3

The Holy Spirit (Holy Ghost)

Acts 1 and 2 tell of Jesus explaining to the disciples about the Holy Spirit (another helper) coming. The disciples didn't understand, but at this point in Acts, they are filled with the Holy Spirit, and amazing feats started to happen. During this time, Peter, a simple fisherman, knowing he had been filled with this helper (this Holy Spirit), stood and spoke such a beautiful plea for Jesus and His path for all their lives. They listened, and so many followed that day.

Peter gave this instruction to them. "Repent, and be baptized every one of you in the name of Jesus Christ for the remission of sins, and ye shall receive the gift of the Holy Ghost" (Acts 2:38 KJV).

So who or what is the Holy Spirit (Holy Ghost)? The Holy Spirit is God's presence. It is God in spirit form. It is our gift from God to help guide us if we listen. He is our conscience, our voice of intercession to God when we don't have the words.

I would also like to make note here that I do not believe baptism is part our salvation. Confessing our sins, believing in Jesus as God's Son, and committing our obedience to following Him is what we need for salvation. I do believe baptism is an important part of our acknowledging to the world that we are now a believer and follower of Jesus Christ. It is our symbol (our picture) of death and being raised to new life like Jesus was. It is explained well in Romans 6:4–7. But it does take salvation to receive the Holy Spirit.

And in the same way, by our faith, the Holy Spirit helps us with our daily problems and in our praying. For we don't even know what we should pray for, nor how to pray as we should. But the Holy Spirit prays for us with such feeling that it cannot be expressed in words (Romans 8:26 LB).

So where does the Holy Spirit come from, and where did it originate? Jesus says, "If you love me, you will obey my commands. I will ask the Father, and he will give you another helper who will be with you forever."

That helper is the Spirit of Truth. The world cannot accept Him because it doesn't see or know Him. You know Him because He lives with you and will be in you (John 14:15–17 GW). And Paul says,

> In Him, you also, after listening to the message of truth, the gospel of your salvation-having also believed, you were sealed in Him with the Holy Spirit of promise, who is given as a pledge of our inheritance, with a view to the redemption of God's own possession, to the praise of His glory. (Ephesians 1:13–14 NASB)

This verse tells us when we first get to meet the Holy Spirit. And the ESV version of the Bible translates the Holy Spirit from "a pledge of our inheritance, with a view to the redemption of God's own possession" as "the guarantee of our inheritance until we acquire possession of it."

Both versions are "to the praise of His glory." And we also know that the Holy Spirit, God's Spirit, was there in the beginning with God. "And the earth was without form, and void; and darkness was upon the face of the deep. And the spirit of God moved upon the face of the waters" (Genesis 1:2 KJV).

So what does the Holy Spirit do for us and with us exactly? We live for God through Jesus and the Holy Spirit. "For the kingdom of God is not eating and drinking, but righteousness and peace and joy in the Holy Spirit. For he who in this way serves Christ is acceptable to God and approved by men" (Romans 14:17–18 NASB).

"And we know For the flesh sets its desire against the Spirit, and the Spirit against the flesh; for these are in opposition to one another, so that you may not do the things that you please" (Galatians 5:16–17 NASB). "But the fruit of the Spirit is love, joy, peace, patience, kindness, goodness, faithfulness, gentleness, self-control; against such things there is no law" (Galatians 5:22–23 NASB).

Don't we all want these gifts the Holy Spirit offers? And what does the Spirit do for our prayers? We know from the verse listed above, Romans 8:26, that the Holy Spirit fills in where our words are weak or nonexistent, when we just don't know what to say but our heart has the need to pray.

A good friend of ours tells a story of driving on a trip with his family. He got the last-minute notion to make a different turn than he'd planned. Because of it, they were detained in traffic only for a few seconds, but he was not too happy about it. We've all been there.

Right after they got back to moving on the highway and the traffic speed resumed to normal, he looked in his rearview mirror, and right behind him evolved a sight like something you would see in a movie! He said it looked like it happened in slow motion. There, right behind him, an eighteen-wheeler was swerving into another car, parts started going everywhere, and other cars started thrashing into the wreck. And they were almost a part of it all! If it hadn't been for his notion to take a different turn and get delayed for those very few seconds, they would've been the car hit by the eighteen-wheeler.

Luck? Coincidence? The Holy Spirit?

- Luck: chance; fortune (Webster's)
- Coincidence: accidental occurrence together of events (Webster's)
- Holy Spirit (or Ghost): third person of the Trinity (Webster's)

Which do you think? Have you ever happened on a situation where you were able to help someone in a way or place you hadn't expected? Maybe you hadn't even planned on being there. Ever taken a notion to do or go somewhere you hadn't planned, only to save yourself from a hard situation? Maybe it was a wreck, a medical emergency, or a time you gave unexpected encouragement. Perhaps you held a hand in a time of crisis. Ever thought about sharing God during these moments? What He did and does for you? Do you think these situations were a coincidence or maybe just luck? Could it have been the Holy Spirit?

Before you decide something is luck or coincidence, think about it. Could it be intervention of a supernatural God or a super Holy Spirit? I bet you'll start to discover that it is. There is no chance, coincidence, or accident with God. He sees and knows everything. And everything is for a reason and a purpose. And God is clear.

David wrote in his book of Psalm, "Where can I go from your Spirit? Where can I flee from your presence? If I go up to the heavens, you are there; if I made my bed in the depths, you are there. If I rise on the wings of the dawn, if I settle on the far side of the sea, even there your hand will guide me, your right hand will hold me fast" (Psalm 139:7–10 NIV). Beautiful, reassuring, and promising. Thank You, God. Thank You, Jesus. Thank You, Holy Spirit!

We don't like it when someone else gets credit for something we've done, whether it's through our jobs, home life, or some other way we have excelled. It doesn't endure us to this person or make us want to be closer to him or her in a loving relationship when he or she has taken our credit, our glory.

So why do we think God would be any different? We're all made in His image. He gives to us according to what we've done, again through our jobs, home life, or some other way we have excelled. And we should give Him credit and glory the same way and much more so. After all, like I said, everything comes from Him. Does it not? Read 1 Corinthians 3:8, 2 Corinthians 5:10, Revelation 2:23, and Revelation 22:12.

My husband has gotten bold about witnessing, sharing Jesus, with others at random places. It amazes me some of the places God gives him opportunity and the time both him and the other person will spend talking. He used to not do this.

He jokes and says, "What do I have to lose? I'm sixty-five-plus-years-old now."

But I know it's the Holy Spirit speaking, nudging him, and

he's more in tune to listen and obey now. I don't believe in luck or coincidence anymore. It's all too coincidental! It has to be the Holy Spirit guiding our paths and moving our moments to just the right timing if we listen and obey. We have to be in tune to the Holy Spirit speaking in our lives.

Sometimes we write off these occurrences as luck and coincidence. If we recognized these instances as being the Holy Spirit changing our plans, think of the power we'd be given and the results we could be a part of. "And divided tongues as of fire appeared to them and rested on each one of them. And they were all filled with the Holy Spirit and began to speak in other tongues as the Spirit gave them utterance" (Acts 2:3–4 ESV).

Even Jesus was filled and led by the Holy Spirit, as we're told in Luke 4:1. There are more instances of the Holy Spirit's guiding power in the Bible. Isaiah 61:1 (NASB) says, "The Spirit of the Lord God is upon me, because the Lord has anointed me to bring good news to the afflicted; He has sent me to bind up the brokenhearted, to proclaim liberty to captives, and freedom to prisoners."

Isaiah was written before Jesus was born, so we know the Holy Spirit was there before Jesus. And we read above that the Holy Spirit was there in the beginning, so we know, wherever God was and is, there was and is His Spirit. We have to believe and follow Jesus and follow God's commandments to have the power of the Holy Spirit.

And lastly, I believe the most significant, powerful, and miraculous work of the Holy Spirit is Luke 1:34–35 (ESV). "And Mary said to the angel, 'How will this be since I am a virgin?' And the angel answered her, 'The Holy Spirit will come upon you, and the power of the Most High will overshadow you; therefore the child to be born will be called 'holy'—the Son of God.'"

What do you now understand more about the Holy Spirit?

_____

_____

_____

_____

_____

_____

_____

What experiences in your life can you now see were from the Holy Spirit?

_____

_____

_____

_____

_____

_____

_____

_____

_____

_____

"But you will receive power when the Holy Spirit comes on you; and you will be my witnesses in Jerusalem, and in all Judea and Samaria, and to the ends of the earth" (Acts 1:8 NIV).

Chapter 4

The Trinity

When our children were growing up, we would take ski trips to Colorado and New Mexico. There was one place we went to in New Mexico. As we drove around the last turn on the road to the resort, we would drive by a lake. It was a beautiful lake with the mountains behind, and it was always at least half frozen. This one particular trip, the lake was mostly frozen, but as we went around the bend, the sun started to come out, and the temperature started to rise only slightly.

It made for such a beautiful evaporation coming up off the partially frozen water, and you could feel the humidity fill the air. I think this is a fitting example of a confusing concept, the Trinity, and I felt like I saw it firsthand that day, even if this example were not mine originally.

If we think of God as the liquid water, so vast and free-flowing, Jesus as the solid frozen water, and the Holy Spirit as the gas form, we see God and Jesus being formed in together like the water freezing, hence being solid and liquid together. The evaporation or humidity is like the Holy Spirit, being lifted and spread into everything and everyone, once they have Jesus in his or her heart.

I also like to think of it this way. God is the liquid being poured out to cover all. Jesus came to earth as solid form but always remains with God, as is seen from the example of the water as it melts. The water never separates; it only changes its form. The Holy Spirit is like the evaporation from the water that fills the air. And we all know water evaporated returns to water in condensation. Therefore, any way you put the three together, you have the Trinity, "all in one and one in all," like we say in sports. It is hard to comprehend but so comforting and strengthening when you do understand. We are never alone and without love, hope, and guidance.

I know a sweet man who talks about not being able to wrap his mind around some of these concepts of God. The human mind was not made or meant to wrap around and understand God. We don't have to. We only have to have faith that God has it all covered. That's why He is God and we are not. And we have to believe in Him, Jesus, and His Spirit. "But the Helper, the Holy Spirit, whom the Father will send in my name, he will teach you all things and bring to your remembrance all that I have said to you" (John 14:26 ESV).

> But you, beloved, building yourselves up in your most holy faith and praying in the Holy Spirit, keep yourselves in the love of God, waiting for the mercy of our Lord Jesus Christ that leads to eternal life. And have mercy on those who doubt; save others by snatching them out of the fire; to others show mercy with fear, hating even the garment stained by the flesh. (Jude 20–23 ESV)

We may not be able to wrap our minds around the concepts. We may not be able to understand all God does and why. We may have a hard time believing the miracles of Jesus and the thought of an invisible spirit guiding our every move, but we should be able to understand and believe in faith. After all, we have faith in all sorts of things. We believe in the air we breathe. We believe the sun will come up in the morning and go down in the evening. We believe that gravity will hold us to the ground and that our earth is constant in its position in the universe.

So why is it so hard to believe in the Trinity? And why is it hard to believe that God loves us and gives us purpose and meaning to our lives? I implore you to try living Jude 20–23. Pray. Constantly seek God's love in all you do. Wait upon Jesus and His mercy for you, and then give the same forgiving mercy to others. Again pray.

This thing of being a believer is like a marriage proposal. In fact, Revelation 19:7–9 talks of Jesus as the bridegroom and we (the church), the believers of Jesus, as the bride. We get on our knees and ask God and Jesus to forgive us, and then we are joined with Him in a never-ending bond and receive an intimate, confident, loving guide, the Holy Spirit, an always present divine influence in our daily, moment-by-moment life, all from a loving heavenly Father, God (Ephesians 3).

> And you shall know that I am in the midst of Israel, that I am the Lord your God, and My people shall never again be put to shame. It shall come to pass after this that I will pour out My Spirit upon all flesh, your sons and your daughters shall prophesy; your old men shall dream dreams, and your young men shall see visions, even upon the servants and the maids I will, in those days, pour out of My Spirit. (Joel 2:27–29, 32 ML)

But everyone who calls upon the name of the Lord shall be saved. Jesus instructs us about what to do once we have Him and the Spirit. He is a good husband (Isaiah 54:5; Revelation 19:7–9).

"But I will send you the Comforter—the Holy Spirit, the source of all truth. He will come to you from the Father and will tell you all about me. And you also must tell everyone about me, because you have been with me from the beginning" (John 15:26–27 LB).

"The grace of the Lord Jesus Christ and the love of God and the fellowship of the Holy Spirit be with you all" (2 Corinthians 13:14 ESV).

What is your understanding now of the Trinity?

_____

_____

_____

_____

_____

_____

_____

_____

_____

_____

How is it different from what you thought before?

_____

_____

_____

_____

_____

_____

_____

_____

To bash our God
Is disrespect.
To lift His name
Down low,
It makes our skies
Gray again.
And our rolling plains
Grow mold.

We have to stand
And lift our voice.
We have to get in tune
And show we're together
In all we do,
To grow old without
The gloom.

So do not bash this God
Of mine.
He wants to be
Yours too.
He'll make the world
Great again,
No matter what
You do.

Introduction to Section 2

𝒞xpectations

What is expected? Judas, not Iscariot, said to him, "Lord, how is it that you will manifest yourself to us, and not to the world?" Jesus answered him, "If anyone loves me, he will keep my word, and my Father will love him, and we will come to him and make our home with him" (John 14:22–23 ESV).

Once we know what to do since we know about the Trinity, we have to check our hearts to move forward. If we've accepted and believed Jesus and asked Him into our hearts, it's time to check our hearts to see where we stand and where we need to improve or grow. It's really very simple, but we have put words on a simple act and made it difficult and confusing to understand—words like *ask*, *accept*, *confess*, and *commit*.

Simply put, Jesus says "Follow me." All words aside, we believe who Jesus is, why He came, and what He does for us. We live for Him and follow Him and His instructions. I hope and pray for you that God will clarify any doubts or questions you have concerning salvation. "From that time Jesus began to preach, and to say, Repent: for the kingdom of heaven is at hand ... And later; And he saith unto them, Follow me, and I will make you fishers of men (Matthew 4:17, 19 KJV).

Jesus tells a parable in Mark 4 about the sower and the different soils. These help us see where our hearts are. We set the scene by the sea, and Jesus gets into a boat with a whole crowd of much diversity on the land beside where He was. He said to them,

> "Listen! Behold a sower went out to sow. And as he sowed, some seed fell along the path, and the birds came and devoured it. Other seed fell on rocky ground, where it did not have much soil, and immediately it sprang up, since it had no depth of soil. And when the sun rose, it was scorched, and since it had no root, it withered away. Other seed fell among thorns, and the thorns grew up and choked it, and it yielded no grain. And other seeds fell into good soil and produced grain, growing up and increasing and yielding thirtyfold." And he said, "He who has ears to hear, let him hear." (Mark 4:1–10 ESV)

The birds at the beginning of this parable represent Satan and how quickly He is to snatch those people without roots, a firm foundation, a knowledge of God, and the love in their hearts to follow Him. The seed that sprang up—but was scorched from the sun since it had no roots—is like us with empty, hollow hearts, having no depth. The seeds choked out by the thorns are like us who are distracted, having our attention elsewhere. The seeds that fell into good soil and produced grain are the fruitful hearts. Jesus starts and ends this part of the parable with "listen" and "he who has ears let him hear."

"Ears to hear" represents a heart who is not hardened but receptive and ready to hear God's Word and act on it, therefore giving God glory. Where is your heart today? When checking our hearts, we must look into our emotions and attitudes. What do you think about the most? Wherever your thoughts and mind are, that's where your heart will dwell. What are the memories you are fond of and frequently recall? Are they happy, sad, sweet, or mad memories? What emotions or attitudes do they cause you to express? Maybe it's not memories but something you're going through now.

"Put off your old nature which belongs to your former manner of life and is corrupt through deceitful lusts, and be renewed in the spirit of your minds, and put on the new nature, created after the likeness of God in true righteousness and holiness" (Ephesians 4:22–24 RSV).

Oswald Chambers (1874–1917) said, "The bedrock of Christianity is repentance." You can't have one without the other.

So what are the expectations of and for a believer? What are the conditions of being a believer, or are there any? Where is God's love in this big picture? Where is your love? The first section was a refresher for these next two. We will now dive into what God wants us to do for Him and what He gives us.

When I use the word *expectations*, it's meant as a good, positive action. The definition of expectation is a thing looked forward to, a prospect of future good or profit. This doesn't sound like something we would not want, so why are we fearful and question God's expectations? I hope and pray this section calms your fears and answers your questions. This life is not for ourselves. It's not about dying for God. It's all about living for God, and the rewards when we do this are the greatest! "For to me, to live is Christ, and to die is gain" (Philippians 1:21 NASB).

We know our greatest rewards come in heaven and just getting to go to heaven, so why don't we get started preparing for that part of our life now? That is what God wants, and He's going to be doing that with us anyway. God gets our attention in so many ways, through His Word and other people, and sometimes He lets us get so messed up in our own choices that we have to turn to Him.

> Then the angel of the Lord came again and touched him and said, "Get up and eat some more, for there is a long journey ahead of you." So he got up and ate and drank, and the food gave him enough strength to travel forty days and forty nights to Mount Horeb, the mountain of God, where he lived in a cave. But the Lord said to him, "What are you doing here, Elijah?" He replied, "I have worked very hard for the Lord God of the heavens; but the people of Israel have broken their covenant with you and torn down your altars and killed your prophets, and only I am left; and now

they are trying to kill me, too." "Go out and stand before me on the mountain," the Lord told him. And as Elijah stood there the Lord passed by, and a mighty windstorm hit the mountain; it was such a terrible blast that the rocks were torn loose, but the Lord was not in the wind. After the wind, there was an earthquake, but the Lord was not in the earthquake. And after the earthquake, there was a fire, but the Lord was not in the fire. And after the fire, there was the sound of a gentle whisper. When Elijah heard it, he wrapped his face in his scarf and went out and stood at the entrance of the cave. And a voice said, "Why are you here, Elijah?" He replied again, "I have been working very hard for the Lord God of the armies of heaven, but the people have broken their covenant and have torn down your alters; they have killed every one of your prophets except me; and now they are trying to kill me, too." (1 Kings 19:7–14 LB)

And God's response in 1 Kings 19:15–18 states that He whispers and reveals Himself through new souls, new voices, and new Christians. And we also see from these verses that God is still in control of who those new Christians will be. We may never know on this earth how we have helped someone or have been helped ourselves. We're only to be ready to take up our cross and follow Him daily to our jobs, with our families and friends, and, yes, if He calls, to other places, towns, and countries. What I really love about this story is that God doesn't always show Himself and His will in great and dramatic ways but sometimes in ways as soft as a whisper.

What excuse are you giving God over and over? Maybe you're just not hearing Him. Elijah was looking for words, instruction from God, and he was looking in the wind, the earthquake, and the fire, but God wasn't talking through these. His Word, His instruction, came softly afterward in a whisper for Israel and us to see and hear His softness and gentleness.

Elijah was disappointed and felt hopelessness because of Israel and didn't see what God had just done and would do. God would do the dealing with Israel; Elijah needed to only do what God told him to do. Israel wasn't Elijah's situation to contend with.

We, like Elijah, look for God in the "big things," the "big picture," and miss so many of His really "big blessings" from our narrowed insight, foresight, and hindsight. We have to be quiet and still to hear His whispering (Psalm 46:10).

Now let's look at and open up our thoughts. What big church words are you most afraid of? Again, this is for your and God's eyes only.

_____

_____

_____

_____

_____

_____

_____

_____

_____

_____

Do we think of God as conditional or unconditional? Which way do you think He loves us? Don't use the church thoughts but your thoughts.

_____

_____

_____

_____

_____

_____

_____

_____

_____

Are you a conditional or unconditional person? How are you toward your family, friends, and God? Be honest.

_____

_____

_____

_____

_____

_____

_____

_____

_____

_____

What does a "life as a believer" mean to you?

_____

_____

_____

_____

_____

_____

_____

_____

I hope this all becomes very clear to you. We get caught up with words and miss what's really important to our lives, which are our actions. It's not okay to do whatever you want because you're "saved."

Chapter 5

God's Conditions and Unconditional Love

First, we need to look at the meaning of the words *unconditional* and *conditional*. We are using these words as pertaining to God's love and our love.

- Unconditional: having no limits or required reactions for an action; someone does something without expecting anything in return
- Conditional: having terms, stipulations, or expectations in receiving something in return for an action

Unconditional doesn't mean we never have to do anything for God's salvation, His saving grace, and His love for eternity. The condition is that you turn from sin, your evil ways. Then repent, ask forgiveness for those sins, believe Jesus is His Son, and ask Jesus into your heart. That doesn't mean you'll never sin again or do everything perfectly, never falling back into your old ways.

I know I did, but that's where God's unconditional love comes in. He still loves us! And then He has something for us to do in return. You could think of this as a condition since Webster's describes condition as a prerequisite and to make accustomed to. The something, job, or privilege God has for us is to help Him in growing His kingdom and fighting Satan as well as assisting Him to spread the wonderful news about Jesus and eternity in heaven.

Understanding is all about how you look at conditional and unconditional. Jesus has a free gift. It's just like a parent loves his or her child unconditionally, or so I hope so, meaning you love your child no matter what he or she does, but there is behavior you hope he or she will demonstrate.

This same example applies to us with our heavenly Father. He loves us unconditionally, but there is behavior He hopes we'll demonstrate. God's salvation is not conditional, but if your heart is truly following Jesus, you'll have the desire, the need, to obey. So there is a condition to receiving unconditional grace and love from God.

The condition is accepting and believing in Jesus. So what about after we accept Jesus? Are there unconditional or conditional responses, expectations, or requirements then? I think this is how some denominations believe salvation is about works, but it's not (Ephesians 2:8–9). The works come out of that desire and need to share what He has done for you.

Before I go any further, there is one thing that really bothers me, our use of words in our Christian walk with God. Actually and interestingly, even the word *Christian* is one that bothers me. Do you know this word appears only three times in the Bible? It appears in Acts 11:26 and 26:28 and 1 Peter 4:16.

I believe it is a grave danger, pun intended, how we throw around words and their meaning. This walk of ours is not about being open-minded. It's about being Christian, Jesus Christ like-minded. This section will define some of our misused words as a believer and help us define them so we can share in a Jesus Christ-like way. It grieves me to think some believers may be falling complacent or lukewarm or haven't even truly believed altogether because of their misunderstanding of certain words.

Jesus said, "I know your works: you are neither cold nor hot. Would that you were either cold or hot! So, because you are lukewarm, and neither hot nor cold, I will spit you out of my mouth" (Revelation 3:15–16 ESV). And I'm just as guilty.

These are some of the words we need to clarify for a believer, and the definitions given are how they pertain to a believer's life.

- Christian: name given to the followers of Jesus.
  - o It was first used at Antioch to distinguish the disciples from others. Interestingly this name only appears three times in the New Testament (Acts 11:26, 26:28; 1 Peter 4:16).

- Believe: the root word from where the word *faith* is derived.
  - o It means faith, assurance, firm persuasion, or firm conviction. In early Greek, *believe* means to put your trust, your faith, in something or someone.

Let me note here, as I was mentioning above, that I will refer to the word *believer* instead of *Christian* in this book, as pertaining to me and you if you are a believer. I know from experience that some people will associate the word *Christian* with certain denominations. I am a believer of Jesus Christ and who He is and what He did and does! I also know Jesus's salvation is open to all people, not just certain denominations. I want this to be totally clear so this is why I will use the word *believer* throughout this book for those of us who have followed Jesus Christ.

- Complacent: self-satisfied; pleased with oneself, often without awareness of some potential danger or defect.

Complacency is a grave danger (pun not intended but definitely fits) for some believers, so I'm giving you some verses to better understand this: Deuteronomy 8:14, 2 Chronicles 20:33, Proverbs 1:32, and Luke 12:18–21.

- Lukewarm: indifferent; showing little enthusiasm.
  - o This is just as dangerous for a believer as being complacent (Revelation 3:16).

- Faith: a system of religious belief; the obligation of loyalty to a person, promise, engagement, and so on; the observance of this obligation; complete trust or confidence in someone or something; strong belief in God.
- Walk: to conduct oneself in a particular manner; pursue a particular course of life.
- Guidance: leadership; direction; advice or counseling; something that guides.
- Reveal: to make known; disclose; an act or instance of revealing; revelation; disclosure.
- Righteous: morally right or justifiable; virtuous; absolutely genuine or wonderful.
- Glory: adoring praise or worshipful thanksgiving; the splendor and bliss of heaven.
- Salvation: deliverance from the power and penalty of sin; redemption.
- Redemption: deliverance; rescue; atonement for guilt; repurchase, as of something sold.
- Saved: to deliver from the power and consequences of sin; to keep from being lost.
- Repentance: deep sorrow for a past sin, wrongdoing, or the like; regret for any past action; a change of mind with sorrow for something done and a wish that it was undone.
- Perfect: conforming absolutely to the description or definition of an ideal type; make flawless or faultless.
- Blameless: free from or not deserving blame; guiltless.
- Just: guided by truth, reason, justice, and fairness; righteous.
- Follow: go or come after (a person or thing proceeding ahead); to go in the same direction as a road, path, and so on (dictionary.cambridge.org); to understand something as it is being said or done; understand.
- Accept: to take or receive; receive with approval or favor; to respond or answer affirmatively to.
- Ask: call for an answer to; inquire of or about; request; invite.

I believe it's very important to note here that, although we may ask Jesus to come into our hearts, we have to ask ourselves if we have truly accepted Him and believe who He is and know without a doubt that we have received God's grace, forgiveness, and inheritance of eternity in heaven. A good example to clarify this is in how we teach our children to ask for something, "What do you say?" or "What's the magic word?" They will eventually say *please*, the magic word, but is it in their hearts?

- Church: the whole body of Christian believers; the people who God has called to serve Him.
  - We are the church. We are His people. (So much of the time today, we use the term *church* for a building or facility.)

- Testimony: an open declaration or profession, as of faith.
  - Interestingly, in biblical times, *test* was used to tell about Jesus. We use it to tell about our story, hopefully, including Jesus and the blessing we've received.

- Blessing: a special favor, mercy, or benefit; a favor or gift bestowed by God, thereby bringing happiness; praise; devotion; worship; especially grace said before a meal.
  - God's first blessing was Genesis 1:22. The second was Genesis 1:28. These blessings were given firstly on the fifth day to the creatures of the seas and the birds. The second was on the sixth day to Adam and Eve. Both blessings were to be fruitful and multiply and to fill the earth.)

- Grace: favor or goodwill; mercy; clemency; pardon; the freely given, unmerited favor and love of God.
- Gospel: the teaching or revelation of Christ.
  - It originally meant "good news" or the Christian message, but it later was used for the books containing the message.

- Disciple: one of twelve personal followers of Christ; any followers of Christ; a person who is a pupil or an adherent of the doctrines of another; to teach; train.

Read these next verses and notice their difference and yet their sameness from different translations:

- "These are the generations of Noah: Noah was a just man and perfect in his generations, and Noah walked with God" (Genesis 6:9 KJV).
- "These are the generations of Noah. Noah was a righteous men, blameless in his generation. Noah walked with God" (Genesis 6:9 ESV).
- "And when Abram was ninety years old and nine, the Lord appeared to Abram, and said unto him, I am the Almighty God; walk before me, and be thou perfect" (Genesis 17:1 KJV).
- "When Abram was ninety-nine years old the Lord appeared to Abram and said to him, I am God Almighty, walk before me, and be blameless" (Genesis 17:1 ESV).

These two sets of verses basically say the same thing, but in some verses, changing one to two words looks, to me, like some of the importance to God is lost. Notice the definitions of *perfect* and *blameless*. Is there a slight difference?

In other words, do we ever think and hear about being perfect in God's thoughts of us? Being blameless is great and wonderful, but I'd rather be perfect! You? I believe it is very important for us to really understand how God views us to be able to live a believer's life without any complacency or becoming lukewarm. When we get that job promotion or that loving hug from our child because we did something pleasing for them, doesn't it make us want to do even more? The same is true for our walk with God. When we know how happy and pleased He is and how much He values us, it should make us want to do more.

And these next two translations appear to have moved the placement of sin from the mother to the child:

- "Behold, I was shapen in iniquity; and in sin did my mother conceive me" (Psalm 51:5 KJV).
- "Surely I was sinful at birth, sinful from the time my mother conceived me" (Psalm 51:5 NIV).

Both verses have truth. David is lamenting to God over his own sinfulness and that his sinfulness started at conception, not just when he was born. But this does bring up another important condition of ours, to know God's Word (Psalm 119:105; Proverbs 7:2–3; Matthew 4:4; Romans 15:4; Ephesians 6:17; Hebrews 4:12; 2 Timothy 3:16–17).

When my cousin and I got together as kids, she would always beg me for some of my soda pop, as we used to call soft drinks.

She would say, "If you don't give me some, I won't be your friend."

I used to always ponder this as I gave in. I would think, *You're my cousin. You have to be my friend.* I knew she would still love me, but there was a condition to the friendship.

God loves us always, everyone, not just believers. But to be His friend, His child, to have a relationship with Him, there is a condition, an action you have to do, a deed you have to take.

He's saying, "I want to be your friend, but I can't until you do something for me."

God's love is unconditional, but it comes personally, individually, to each of us by a condition. I would learn years later that my cousin wasn't allowed soda pop and always wanted mine because of a health issue. So what I always gave her was bad for her. God's conditions, His wants and desires, are always for our best. His desires better, bless, and especially further our lives, even past our life here on earth.

So does God get what He wants? He should, and it should be easy. It's all good for us. He wants to make us perfect as we walk with Him. I loved this cousin so I would do whatever she wanted.

So I ask, "Do you love God enough to do whatever He wants? Enough to do His conditions? To accept Jesus and live for Him?"

You might ask, "How do I know if I love God?"

I ask you, "How do you know you don't love God?"

It only takes a step of faith! Jesus did a very conditional act of dying on a cross for us because He loved us unconditionally and

His mercy was unconditional. And we do a conditional act of a prayer of repentance, confessing our sins and acknowledging that we believe Jesus died a horrendous death for those sins and that we commit our lives to living for Him. Our hearts are then filled with the unconditional love, support, and guidance of His Holy Spirit.

Jesus didn't specifically call us to this action while He was on the cross, but lots of verses in God's Word mention what we're to do for His salvation and His saving grace and how we then treat others. Some are the Ten Commandments and the Love Chapter of 1 Corinthians 13.

Do you not know that you are God's temple and that God's Spirit dwells in you? If anyone destroys God's temple, God will destroy him. For God's temple is holy, and you are that temple (1 Corinthians 3:16 RS).

How do you view God's love now?

_____

_____

_____

_____

_____

_____

_____

_____

_____

_____

How do you view yourself from God's perspective now?

_____

_____

_____

_____

_____

_____

_____

_____

_____

"I will give thanks to You, for I am fearfully and wonderfully made; Wonderful are Your works, And my soul knows it very well" (Psalm 139:14 NASB).

Chapter 6

Our Conditions and Unconditional Love

In the last chapter, we looked at ourselves from God's view, His perspective. In this chapter, we're going to look at ourselves from our view, our perspective. Are we conditional or unconditional to our friends and family? Which are we to God?

We sometimes are hesitant to accept Jesus, to walk the aisle at a church, or to just get on our knees to pray because we are such conditional people. We don't know or understand the meaning and feeling of unconditional. Our society teaches us that we do to receive. We expect from others and ourselves. We hesitate because there's something not right in our lives yet or there's some other reason we're waiting on to be answered or fulfilled. We just can't get past the feeling that we must do something first or God must show something first to have salvation.

Don't let the thought of conditional scare you. Repentance is easy and most helpful to you, and it is the most important condition you will ever do. It is an act of the heart. When all other acts can be from the mind and body, so therefore truly conditional, the act of the heart is truly emotional and full of honest expression (Acts 26:15–20). And as is said, "Know that you know that you know!"

"You are my portion, Lord; I have promised to obey your words. I have sought your face with all my heart; be gracious to me according to your promise. I have considered my ways and have turned my steps to your statutes. I will hasten and not delay to obey your commands" (Psalm 119:57–60 NIV).

And it is received by a God full of mercy and grace. "Let us then approach God's throne of grace with confidence, so that we may receive mercy and find grace to help us in our time of need" (Hebrews 4:16 NIV).

The conditions included in God's unconditional grace come from Him within us. He does the changing, mending, and sorting through and returns it with love and His Spirit inside us, in our hearts. Our only condition is to open the door of our heart and let Him in.

So why do we hesitate? We're fearful! We're fearful of failing, not being accepted anymore by the very ones we probably need to be away from anyway, and knowing what God Himself has in store for us to do. We want to be in control. We want to know the plans before they happen so we can decide if that is what we want to do. We want to know what God will do and if He is even going to do something. We expect to know.

So what do we think of when we hear conditional in contrast to unconditional? Wedding vows exclaim unconditional love, but are they? Conditional benefits me, what I want. Unconditional benefits others at no cost to them. You punish your children by showing conditional behavior for their benefit. They do this, so you do that. But when you show them you love them just as much as you did before the act that needed punishment, that's unconditional love.

We're taught to love everyone unconditionally because God loves us unconditionally. Unconditional implies no action is needed, but there are actions needed to live a believer's life to its fullest. Jesus on the cross dying a horrendous death, full of pain and shame, showed the most selfless act full of unconditional love ever recorded. "Then said Jesus, 'Father, forgive them; for they know not what they do.' And they parted his raiment, and cast lots" (Luke 23:34 KJV).

Unconditional acts are so great because they're done from the heart and not for show or gain.

> You shall therefore impress these words of mine on
> your heart and on your soul; and you shall bind them

as a sign on your hand, and they shall be as frontals on your forehead. And you shall teach them to your sons, talking of them when you sit in your house and when you walk along the road and when you lie down and when you rise up (Deuteronomy 11:18-19 NASB).

I can guarantee and testify that, behind every underage drinker is an adult involved, enabling him or her somewhere. The adult has brought alcohol into his or her home within reach or sold it at a store, but there is an adult somewhere who has been a part somehow, even if he or she never intended for a child to be led the wrong way. God expects us to raise our children to know Him and His Word so they'll tell about Him to their children. But sometimes we get too busy with our own concerns and wants, our conditions.

What is your testimony, your words for God, of God, and with God? What will you tell your children? What do you love, and how do you love it, conditionally or unconditionally? The word *agape* is defined as a selfless, sacrificial, and unconditional love. It is used to refer to the highest form of love. This is how God loves us and is also used for the love Jesus had for His Father and followers. It means immeasurable and incomparable.

God gives this love without condition to us who are so undeserving (John 3:16, 13:35, 14:21, 17:23; 1 Corinthians 3:16; 1 John 4:8). Our conditions include "believe in Him," "have love for one another," "have God's commands and keep them," "so that the world may know," "lay down our lives for our brothers," and again "love!"

God gives us. "The Lord appeared to him from far away. 'I have loved you with an everlasting love; therefore I have continued my faithfulness to you'" (Jeremiah 31:3 ESV).

And we give. "And he said, 'What comes out of a person is what defiles him. For from within, out of the heart of man, come evil thoughts, sexual immorality, theft, murder, adultery, coveting, wickedness, deceit, sensuality, envy, slander, pride, foolishness. All these evil things come from within, and they defile a person'" (Mark 7:20-23 ESV).

What conditions do you need to give up?

_____

_____

_____

_____

_____

_____

_____

_____

Do you need to recheck your heart for the urging drive to do God's conditions? What makes you hesitate?

_____

_____

_____

_____

_____

_____

_____

_____

_____

What words do you understand differently now?

_____

_____

_____

_____

_____

_____

_____

_____

Chapter 7

Our Life as a Believer

What does a life as a believer look like? What are we supposed to be doing? We've looked at God and ourselves in this section, and now we'll apply it to our lives. When we love God as He loves us, we want to go, do, share, witness, minister, and tell the world. We know this by the overwhelming feelings of joy, excitement, success, love, and knowledge of God. Our life becomes clear, along with what the ultimate reason and purpose is. This life of ours on earth takes a back seat to the abundant life God promises and has planned for us in heaven, and we want everyone else to know and have that promise as well.

So what do we know about the situations and everyday life as a believer that we go through? Do we know where our hearts are during these times and all the other moments? Do we rely on God constantly or occasionally? How do we ask Him to help us? When do we ask Him to help us? Where are our hearts when we are asking or going to Him? Are we pleading, begging, thanking, praising, conversing, blaming, blaspheming, loving, hating, or questioning?

It's important to know that we don't have to have a college-plus education to understand God's Word. If we wait until we feel knowledgeable, we'd never share His gospel, His good news. God's not waiting on us to be knowledgeable. He is all knowledge. He's waiting on us to be willing and obedient to what He has to tell us. He's waiting on our commitment.

In Matthew 9:9, Jesus commands Matthew to "follow Me." It is a command, but it means to walk beside and with Him. Matthew 8:22 shows we are to be committed to Him and our new family of faith more than anyone or anything else on this earth. So one way our life is to be as a believer is to take Jesus wherever we go, "follow Him" and His commands, being committed to having Him with us always (Joshua 1:9; Psalm 139:7–12; Isaiah 43:2; Zephaniah 3:17). We do this mainly and mostly, actually consistently, through prayer.

Our commitment to God is to pray constantly and "see that none render evil for evil unto any man; but ever follow that which is good, both among yourselves, and to all men. Rejoice evermore. Pray without ceasing. In everything give thanks: for this is the will of God in Christ Jesus concerning you" (1 Thessalonians 5:15–18 KJV).

A life of a believer includes a commitment to pray without ceasing, with thanksgiving and rejoicing. It includes doing unto others as we want them to do to us (Luke 6:31) and never being unreliable or untrustworthy. We are to be wise in the areas of opportunities God gives us, no matter if it's a job, home, church, recreation, sports assemblies, and so on.

> Who among you is wise and understanding? Let him show by his good behavior his deeds in the gentleness of wisdom. But if you have bitter jealousy and selfish ambition in your heart, do not be arrogant and so lie against the truth. This wisdom is not that which comes down from above, but is earthly, natural, demonic. For where jealousy and selfish ambition exist, there is disorder and every evil thing. But the wisdom from above is first pure, then peaceable, gentle, reasonable, full of mercy and good fruits, unwavering, without hypocrisy. And the seed whose fruit is righteousness is sown in peace by those who make peace. (James 3:13–18 NASB)

And we know more "works of the flesh" are sexual immorality, impurity, sensuality, idolatry, sorcery, enmity, strife, jealousy, fits of anger, rivalries, dissensions, divisions, envy, drunkenness, and orgies (Galatians 5:19–21). And we've all heard of the seven deadly sins of envy, gluttony, greed, lust, pride, sloth, and wrath. These are all listed throughout God's Word. The main thing to know about all of these is the end to Galatians 5:21, which says those who practice these things will not inherit the kingdom of God.

When we follow all the things God has instructed us to do, it makes our purpose, our reason to live for Him, so much more easy and natural. Our witness, our testimony, is evident to all who encounter our lives. Our lives bless them, and God blesses us. Our rewards will come (Luke 6:23). So we prepare our minds and hearts to live for God, letting our light shine (Matthew 5:16), to be the salt of His earth (Matthew 5:13), and to be holy as He is holy!

> Therefore, gird your minds for action, keep sober in spirit, fix your hope completely on the grace to be brought to you at the revelation of Jesus Christ. As obedient children, do not be conformed to the former lusts which were yours in your ignorance, but like the Holy One who called you, be holy yourselves also in all your behavior; because it is written, "You shall be holy, for I am holy." (1 Peter 1:13–16 NASB)

We are to share what we have, love, and never miss the opportunity to tell about the greatest God who gave and gives us everything, whether through our words or deeds. We are to be good stewards of all He gives to us. Our great heavenly Father God passed His love to us through His son. We are to also pass it on. "Tell your children of it, and let your children tell their children, and their children to another generation" (Joel 1:3 ESV).

We are to be mature and listen to God, be content and look to God, and be patient and live with God because He is the ultimate peace giver. He gives us peace of mind knowing all will be okay, peace of body knowing all will feel okay, and peace of spirit knowing where our soul will end up, with Him in heaven forever.

So what is the ultimate reason and purpose? To be ready to do whatever He calls you to do to help Him show others about His love and His kingdom, heaven. Isaiah says in Isaiah 6:8, "Here I am! Send me." Samuel says to God in 1 Samuel 3:10, "Speak, for your servant hears."

Are you ready to go? Are you ready to hear? The urgency to share the name of Jesus and what He is ready to do for all who listen and come to Him is always there. We are the ones He's called to be His stewards, Jude.

And now we will take a test! Just kidding, but sort of. I want you to go down these two lists below. Check the ones you're guilty of, both good and bad. See where you stand and where you need to pray for help and forgiveness to God. Always remember, there is no failing grade, no failures with God. There is only areas for prayer of improvement. Everyone who comes to Him through Jesus Christ passes and passes well! Pray first, and be honest. Remember James 3:14. Don't lie against the truth. God already knows anyway.

Flesh Fruits	**Good Fruits**
Sexual Immorality_____	Love_____
Impurity_____	Joy_____
Gluttony_____	Peace_____
Idolatry_____	Patience_____
Witchcraft_____	Gentleness_____
Hatred_____	Goodness_____
Jealousy_____	Faith_____
Anger_____	Self-control_____
Dissention_____	Sharing_____
Envy_____	Encouragement_____
Drunkenness_____	Forgiving_____
Lying_____	Disciplined_____
Stealing_____	Prayerful_____
Blasphemy_____	Thankful_____

However you did, remember not the things behind you. Look forward because God makes all things new (Isaiah 43:18–20; Philippians 3:13–14). Flesh fruits, you now know, not to do, and good fruits God has already placed inside you to start doing. How? Start praying, and God makes the way, which is our next section.

"He who was seated on the throne said, 'I am making everything new!' Then he said, 'Write this down, for these words are trustworthy and true'" (Revelation 21:5 NIV).

Matthew 28:19 says, "Go therefore." This means we can know and expect that God is with us, the same great, mighty, and all-powerful God that raised Jesus from the dead and put Him upon the same throne with Himself in heaven. We can fulfill what God calls us to do just like Jesus because He goes with us and we go with Him. And we can expect the Holy Spirit to fill our hearts with an overabundance of God's love so much so that our witness is evident. "Praising God and having favor with all the people. And the Lord added to their number day by day those who were being saved" (Acts 2:47 ESV).

We have looked at and learned more about the Trinity, and we've looked at and learned more about what is expected of us and the meaning of some misused and misunderstood Christian believers' words. Now let's look more at what I believe is the greatest blessing our God gives us after salvation through Jesus, His Son. This is the ability and means to converse with Him personally through prayer!

Introduction to Section 3

The Pursuit of Prayer

For the introduction to this section, we will begin with an exercise. List the first five prayers from the Bible that come to your mind and explain them. Remember, this is for yours and God's eyes only, so be honest.

1. _____

_____

_____

_____

_____

2. _____

_____

_____

_____

_____

3. _____

_____

_____

_____

_____

4. _____

_____

_____

_____

_____

5. _____

_____

_____

_____

_____

In Psalm 5, David prays to God to lead him in deliverance and service, and specifically in verse 3, David is praying in the morning, laying his requests before God, and says he will wait "expectantly." This verse helps us understand and put together section 2 with section 3. We will build on this verse through this section.

We ask of ourselves and others, "What are you going to do about it?" when we have a certain situation or incident. Instead ask yourself, and always first, "How am I going to pray about it?" Better still, just start praying. The main thing is to get it out of your determined control and into the One that controls the determined. From our emotions to God's judgement, from our hearts and into His hands, that's how we pray about it.

To love someone, you have to know him or her. To know someone, you have to spend time with him or her. To spend time with God, you have to open and read the Bible, His Word to us, and pray.

So how did you do with the introductory questions? To be honest myself, I had a hard time thinking of five prayers. I had to think about it, and it's okay if you did too. I think most of us would fumble around if we had to come up with five on a moment's notice, and that's just five out of six hundred and fifty! I commend you if you came up with five quickly! This study is focused on helping us see where we have knowledge about God and His Word and where we need to learn more.

In this section, we will look at prayers God gave us as examples, how we are praying now ourselves, and how we can pray differently in the future. Whatever your prayer life is, it can be improved, and improvement only means getting closer to God. Let the blessings begin!

In Exodus, God gave such specific requirements for His tabernacle, not only the measurements and materials used, but down to colors and placements. Exodus 28:36 and 39:30 tells of the crown the priests wore entering the tabernacle. "And they made the plate of the holy crown of pure gold, and wrote upon it a writing, like to the engravings of a signet, HOLINESS TO THE LORD." The priest wore this for himself and for all he represented.

God has also given specifics for the way He wants to be worshipped and prayed to. He did then. He does now. We are His tabernacle! In the Old Testament, the tabernacle was carried with the people wherever they went. We are in the New Testament times with God, Jesus, and the Holy Spirit going wherever we go. We don't have to carry it; it goes with us, inside us, and it is us.

Prayer is the way we hear God and communicate back with God, along with His Word, the Bible. I have to include here that any prayer we pray without acting on what we hear and know God commands is a prayer less heard from God. Our actions have to speak first and foremost.

An example of this is Luke 7:36–50. Jesus is invited to dine with one of the Pharisees. As He is reclining at the table, a very sinful woman from the town enters with expensive perfume and begins weeping and washing Jesus's feet with it. She uses her tears to help wet his feet as she's washing them and then uses her hair to dry them, all the while kissing His feet.

The Pharisee was not in agreement with Jesus allowing this. But Jesus explains through a parable that more action and love is given when we have a bigger debt forgiven. The woman, as horribly sinful as she was, had her debt forgiven that day in such a big way, and she knew it, felt it, and acted on it with great love.

Jesus said to the woman, "Your faith has saved you; go in peace" (Luke 7:50 NIV).

Notice we do not see anything about the sinful woman praying for forgiveness or praying in any fashion to be seen. What we see is that Jesus saw her pain and remorse in her heart as well as her faith and obedience through her actions. So when we pray, hoping God takes action, maybe we should first check our actions toward Him and our hearts. Let's look at our prayers and check if we're hearing what God is saying to us.

Of the five prayers you listed above, which is your favorite?

_____

_____

_____

_____

_____

_____

_____

_____

_____

Do you pray similar to your favorite?

_____

_____

_____

_____

_____

_____

_____

_____

What are your thoughts on how you pray? Are they enough or not enough, short or long, or inclusive or exclusive? Are they at specific times and places?

_____

_____

_____

_____

_____

_____

_____

_____

_____

_____

Are you limiting God through your prayers?

_____

_____

_____

_____

_____

"Rejoice always, pray without ceasing, give thanks in all circumstances; for this is the will of God in Christ Jesus for you" (1 Thessalonians 5:16–18 ESV).

Let's add to our believers' definitions of words from chapter 5. The Hebrew word for *helper* is actually *completer*. God is our helper, our completer.

Prayer is a petition, an entreaty. It is to ask earnestly or beg. It is praise or a religious observance. Webster's says a spiritual communion with God or an object of worship, as in supplication, thanksgiving, adoration, or confession.

Some beautiful understandings of prayer come from quotes.

"For me, prayer, is an aspiration of the heart, it is a simple glance directed to heaven, it is a cry of gratitude and love in the midst of trial as well as joy; finally it is something great, supernatural, which expands my soul and unites me to Jesus" (St. Therese of Liseiux).

"Prayer is, at root, simply paying attention to God" (Dr. Ralph Martin).

Praying is not just an activity, something we make a time and place for, and a point of something to do. These things are wonderful and good, but prayer is so much more. It's a way of life, a second by second in our thoughts always process. It's an attitude, a lifestyle, and the most important to our lives. After all, prayer is all about life and death.

Chapter 8

Past Prayers

Prayer began in Genesis, of course. People had dialogue with God, and before Genesis 4, God actually initiated this Himself (Genesis 3:8–13, 4:9). Adam and Eve conversed with God directly. And we know Adam and Eve had two sons, Cain and Abel. We also know the story about Cain killing Abel from Genesis 4, but how much do we know about their next son, Seth?

> And Adam knew his wife again; and she bare a son, and called his name Seth: For God, said she, hath appointed me another seed instead of Abel, whom Cain slew. And to Seth, to him also there was born a son; and he called his name Enos: then began men to call upon the name of the Lord (Genesis 4:25–26 KJV).

God answered Eve's prayer then, just like He does now, and sometimes He answered in miraculous ways then. And sometimes He answers our prayers in miraculous ways now. Just asking Jesus to be our Savior is a life-changing miracle.

So in Genesis, prayer began, and walking with God continued. I will not list or talk about all the prayers in the Bible because there are 650 listed. I will add there are about 450 answers to prayer recorded, and it's interesting to note the Bible gives us twenty-five of these prayers by Jesus Himself. Did you have trouble thinking of five? We will look at the types of prayers, the postures of prayers, and the way Jesus told us to pray.

Let's look at several types of prayer. We pray of faith (James 5:15). We have the prayer of agreement (Acts 2:42). We pray in petition, to request something, (Philippians 4:6). And I hope we all pray with thanksgiving and in worship to God (Psalm 95:2–6). We give prayers of dedication (Matthew 26:39) and intercession (1 Timothy 2:1). In this verse, Paul is trying to show the importance of praying for all kinds of things and people.

Psalm 51 is a great example of a prayer for forgiveness, and we are to pray in the Spirit. "But you, beloved, building yourselves up on your most holy faith; praying in the Holy Spirit" (Jude 20 NASB).

Who do you tend to pray for the most—others or yourself? When I was young, I didn't think God wanted to hear my wants and needs. I felt selfish praying for these things, so I prayed for others. It took many years for me to understand that God wants to hear from me about me and then everyone else. And it took even more years for me to understand how to do this and actually start doing it.

Let's get honest and open. Our prayer life should be more about God and less about ourselves anyway. Don't misunderstand. God wants our requests. Psalm 5:3 is one of my favorite and one of the most prayed verses. "In the morning, O Lord, you hear my voice; in the morning I lay my requests before you and wait in expectation" (NIV).

We are given examples of how to pray and the importance of their sequence.

And what about the posture of prayer? I have heard from many Bible studies, preachers, individuals, and even movies on the posture I should practice while praying. While every posture is good, the main thing is to pray, and I don't think God is now specific on your body position when compared to your heart position. The most used positions in our culture are sitting (2 Samuel 7:18), standing (Mark 11:25), and kneeling (2 Chronicles 6:13; Daniel 6:10; Luke 22:41, Ephesians 3:14; and more).

Less practiced today but still used in some areas of our world are praying with your face to the ground as Jesus did (Matthew 26:39; Mark 14:35). And Paul urges people to pray with their hands lifted up to God in the heavens (1 Timothy 2:8). What is your normal posture while you pray? Do you use different postures at different times in different places?

Jesus gives us direct instruction on how to pray. Every focus, every main component, and each aspect of how to pray He has given us is simply and shortly listed in Matthew 6:6–13 (NIV). We see the place He directs us to first. We see the first verses are directed toward God. We see that we pray for others. We need to pray for God to bless others, but we also need to pray for God to be blessed first, and we see we're to include ourselves. Let's look at these verses closer.

In verse 6, it reads, "But when you pray, go into your room, close the door and pray to your Father, who is unseen." This verse gives us the where of importance.

Verses 5 and 7, which I have not written out, refer to the hypocrites praying while standing and the pagans babbling on to be heard because of their many words. I believe this is the place and how of importance, but there are many times in the Bible when people prayed in different ways at different places. This is our example when we are praying alone. Think of the times Jesus prayed alone. He would go off by Himself and pray to God.

Verse 9 says, "Our Father in heaven, hallowed be your name." The focus here is to identify God's everlasting glory and indicate that His name is to have all honor. The word *our* is acknowledging the relationship we have with Him. It shows praise and submission to Him and references that He is everything to us.

Verse 10 states, "Your kingdom come." This focus is about God's heaven, our heaven to come with Him in eternity and on earth after we acknowledge and believe Jesus to be God's Son and our Savior from our sins.

"Your will be done, on earth as it is in heaven." This too focuses on God and His desire for our love, loyalty, and devotion. The word *your* in these last two verses focuses on God's sovereign authority and influence in our lives and, again, our submission to Him.

Verse 11 reads, "Give us this day our daily bread." This is referring to our every provision, our every need. And verse 12 states, "And forgive us our debts, as we forgive our debtors." Simply put, we forgive as we're forgiven. And as my preacher son said, "If you think you're not sinning, you don't know what sin is and need to get into God's word," simply put.

Verse 13 says, "And lead us not into temptation, but deliver us from evil." This is praying for God to guide us from Satan, for our eyes and heart to stay focused on Him and not the things of the world. We are constantly battling evil and temptation so this should be a daily, if not hourly or minute-by-minute, prayer.

The King James Version concludes with, "For thine is the kingdom, and the power, and the glory, forever. Amen." Interestingly, this phrase is not in all translations and is even omitted from the early manuscripts, but it is definitely a phrase we need to pray to worship and glorify Him, the powerful and almighty God who gives us everything.

The word *Amen* means "let it be," "so be it," or "truly." Since Jesus ended the Lord's Prayer with it, I believe we should all use it. It's a form of testifying, proclaiming it is God's way as the only or true way. We thought we knew how to pray. Were you "missing the boat," so to say, on a lot of the importance, structure, and knowledge of prayer? Aren't we glad Jesus came walking on the water?

What do you think of your choice prayers now? Do you see them differently? Do you wonder what posture the one praying had or the type of prayer it was? Look back at your five prayers and see if you have different thoughts now?

_____

_____

_____

_____

_____

_____

_____

_____

_____

_____

My five prayer choices were first the Lord's Prayer, especially Matthew 6:6–7 (NASB).

> But you, when you pray, go into your inner room, and when you have shut your door, pray to your Father who is in secret, and your Father who sees in secret will repay you. And when you are praying, do not use meaningless repetition, as the Gentiles do, for they suppose that they will be heard for their many words.

Job, my second choice, is the oldest book in the Bible. Job is a wealthy man, and Satan is asking God if he can test him. Satan causes Job to lose everything and strikes him with a horrible disease. All the while, Job never ceases to praise God and never falters in his devotion to Him. Job 42 is his confessing and asking God to forgive him. This book is a great read for every believer. You've heard the phrase, "Now my eyes see you." It's from Job 42:5. He said it first here.

I remembered Jesus praying to God on the cross and Jesus praying in the gardens, but since Jesus has forty-one prayers recorded in the Bible, I should've been able to remember more. Easily!

I really had to work on my last prayer choice to remember, so don't feel bad if you struggled. Mine was the Prayer of Jabez. I remembered this one's title far more than I remembered the prayer. Do you have the picture? How well are we doing at knowing this great command and great blessing our God gives us? Recall this command and blessing of prayer (Philippians 4:6–7).

> Jabez was more honorable than his brothers. His mother had named him Jabez, saying, "I gave birth to him in pain." Jabez cried out to the God of Israel, "Oh, that you would bless me and enlarge my territory! Let your hand be with me, and keep me from harm so that I will be free from pain." And God granted his request. (1 Chronicles 4:9–10 NIV)

Chapter 9

Present Prayers

What hinders your prayers? Is it something you're harboring in your heart? If I had cherished iniquity in my heart, the Lord would not have listened (Psalm 66:18 ESV). Is it something you've dealt with in your past that has weakened your faith or trust? Maybe it's something you need to let go of and let God handle.

When I was a child, my faith and trust were so broken by man that I harbored hatred and revenge in my heart. When I heard Psalm 66:18 at the age of twenty-two, I realized my prayers were less heard from God, if not unheard altogether. It wouldn't have surprised me if God had turned away from me at that time. I was so focused on my hatred and bitterness, but we know He doesn't turn from us. Blessedly for me, this verse broke my heart toward God, and I had to ask forgiveness for my feelings. The person that read it to me has been my husband for over thirty years.

If we think of our existence, even the nonbeliever would have to concur that a big part includes God, examples being Easter and Christmas, trying to be convincing as to why they don't believe. At those times, they wonder if praying to a God they don't believe in would really help. After all, the Bible is still the number-one bestseller. But for us believers, what is one thing mostly wanted in our own world? Would you say honest communication is one?

What do parents want so much from their children? Would you

say honest communication? We want our kids to communicate with us, to talk with us, and to tell us what's going on. What do we want from our friends? We want them to communicate with us, to talk with us, and to tell us what's going on. What do we want from our spouses and loved ones? We want them to communicate with us, to talk with us, and to tell us what's going on.

God wants the same as us and from us! He wants our communication, to talk with Him and to tell Him what's going on.

You might ask, "If God already knows everything that's going to happen and already knows everyone who's going to be saved, why do we need to pray?"

Are our prayers wasted energy? Or is there a reason to pray even if God already knows all? As a young mother myself, our Sunday school class did a prayer vigil on the lawn of a family whose baby was in the hospital in extremely critical condition. We prayed and prayed.

I wondered these very questions all the time I was praying. "If God already knows what will happen, why pray? What about? What if?"

The baby was miraculously healed in the doctor's eyes. But God already knew this. So why pray? Was the healing of the baby the actual end result, or was it for the healing of our hearts, those of us praying, like me? Was it for our humility, for us to realize just how small we are and how big God is, and for us to turn to Him in submission, love, and gratefulness? I know it was for all of these. God uses prayer in many ways. Ultimately it's to bring our hearts and lives into accordance with His (James 5:13–16).

God is specific with instruction. In Matthew 21, Jesus causes a fig tree to wither and die, which is another topic, but He explains to the disciples when they ask how it withered. "Truly I say to you, if you have faith, and do not doubt, you shall not only do what was done to the fig tree, but even if you say to this mountain, 'Be taken up and cast into the sea,' it shall happen. And everything you ask in prayer, believing, you shall receive" (Matthew 21:21–22 NASB).

Moses believed. Then Moses and Aaron went out from Pharaoh, and Moses cried to the Lord concerning the frogs, which He had inflicted upon Pharaoh. And the Lord did according to the word of

Moses, and the frogs died out of the houses, the courts, and the fields (Exodus 8:12–13 NASB).

In Joshua 9, we read a story of Joshua and his army, who were deceived into alliance with the enemy all because they "did not ask counsel from the Lord" (Joshua 9:14 ESV). Joshua knew the power of communicating with God. He just failed in this situation, but he is still our good and faithful example. In Joshua 10:12–14, Joshua spoke to God in front of Israel, asking God to stop the moon and have the sun stand still. And God did!

Skeptics today may try to excuse this miracle away, but we know it's because Joshua believed and knew who to turn to. God wants to hear from us, and He does answer our prayers. The key is to believe. We have to believe in Jesus first, but we also have to believe in God's power and His sovereign will to want to answer our prayers.

How many times do you pray for something, not believing it will happen? Maybe we're afraid to feel like our prayers aren't answered, so we just don't pray for something. Or we pray, "If it's your will, God," but we never believe He is going to answer or could. Do any of these scenarios fit your present prayer life? Once you get to the attitude and belief in God answering your prayers, you will see the amazement He gives by actually answering them. He is an amazing God!

So the best way to pray in the present is to always be praying in the present. It's a heart attitude, a heart lifestyle. Prayer and the continuation of it are to be always in our hearts. "Rejoice always; pray without ceasing" (1 Thessalonians 5: 16 NASB). This is simply making it a habit that will eventually become a lifestyle, one of going to God before everything you do and as you do everything.

It's a lifestyle of having an ongoing process of Him being in your thoughts, not the thought of calling someone on your phone. You'll be talking to God. Examples are:

- "God, help me do this."
- "God, give me wisdom and knowledge to know what to do."
- "God send me someone to help me."
- "Thank you, God."

- "God, what a beautiful morning."
- "What a sad situation for them, God. Please help them."

And it never ceases. Do you already have these thoughts, these prayers, in your mind? Are they never ceasing? My hatred, revenge, and anger were never ceasing until I prayed to God. Are you fearful or forgetful? Are you afraid God won't hear? Are you afraid of what God might ask of you if you pray? Do you feel awkward praying, in private or public?

I've had many times I was asked to pray and I felt awkward. Praying will come naturally with doing it and keeping in mind what, why, and to whom you're doing it and knowing that He's already and always with you. This is part of that habit I was talking about. It will become so easy and something you don't even have to think about. It will start to come naturally. Prayer will be a part of your lifestyle, just like eating and sleeping.

A story about an awkward moment of prayer for me happened when our grandson was born. I felt pretty at ease with my prayer lifestyle at that time. I was in the hospital maternity ward bathroom, and another lady, very obviously a new grandma like myself, was in there on her cell phone. She was distressed while talking to the other person, to the point of having tears in her eyes.

She finished her call, and I had to ask her if she were okay. She told me the horribly sad story about her new granddaughter having been born with some physical issues from the way she had been in the womb with the cord around her neck, cutting off oxygen flow to parts of her little body and having her legs up over her head during delivery. It was all so sad. They were getting ready to care flight the baby with her son, the new daddy, to a hospital more equipped to help the baby. The new mom would have to join in a few days after she recovered more from the delivery.

What should've been a joyous occasion had turned to something so different so quickly. I told her I'd be praying for her, not knowing if she believed in prayer or not.

She then looked at me and asked, "Can you pray now?"

Of course my first thought was, *Now? Here in the bathroom?*

You think that felt awkward? Blessedly, I was at a point in my prayer lifestyle that the awkwardness was only for a fraction of a second. Thank You, God! So I prayed right there in the bathroom, not even caring if someone walked in. And when I finished, I thought, *That didn't seem awkward at all!*

In fact, it was quite calming and reassuring for her and me. This is where we all need to get to in our prayer life. Where are you as far as prayer being an every moment occurrence, a lifestyle attitude, for you?

I hope and pray this session, this book, will help you get closer to that style of life. I wish I'd learned it sooner. It is an amazing lifestyle! You never have to wait. You don't have to go to a prayer closet or get your phone, and you don't have to rely on your mind to remember to pray for something or someone if it's already and always in your heart.

> But blessed is the man who trusts in the Lord, whose confidence is in him. He will be like a tree planted by the water that sends out its roots by the stream. It does not fear when heat comes; its leaves are always green. It has no worries in a year of drought and never fails to bear fruit. (Jeremiah 17:7–8 NIV)

Chapter 10

Future Prayers and Your Prayer Lifestyle

"You do not have, because you do not ask God" (James 4:2 NIV). James also tells us in chapter 4 that, when we ask and don't receive, it's because our prayers are for our own desires and motives and not for God's desires and motives. We have not submitted ourselves to God and His will for our lives; therefore, our prayers go unanswered.

From our previous two chapters, what are some ways you already see your need to change your prayer lifestyle?

_____

_____

_____

_____

_____

_____

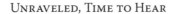

_____

_____

_____

_____

We have learned we need to be praying without ceasing, going to God all the time, actually never being away from Him. We have seen an example of the order to pray with the Lord's Prayer, and we have seen examples of God's people who simply walked with God, communicating with Him at all times. This is what we need to achieve.

So how do we get into this habit so it will become a lifestyle? Why do we need to pray constantly? You might think, like myself and others I've known, _I'm already a believer and going to heaven. So why pray this way?_

The reason is simple: God tells us to. He also gives us His power through prayer for us, those around us, those in our future, and Him, all to further the glory in His coming kingdom, heaven (James 5:16).

First and foremost, you have to admit that you're not already in this habit, this lifestyle. Check yourself to see who you go to first: God or your phone. If you had answers to the question that started this chapter, you already see ways you need improvement. Take notice of what your normal habits are as far as what you do in any and every given situation.

If you're like me, I thought I prayed all the time. It wasn't until I took a challenge that I realized I wasn't. I challenge you to take the same test. It's from a Beth Moore Bible study. She wears a bracelet with an acknowledgement of Jesus on it, a verse or a cross, something that reminds her that she belongs to God. I wear a bracelet or a ring with a verse or a cross. This only works if you wear something visible to you at all times. A necklace won't work because you only see it when you look in the mirror. Men can do this too. There are rings and bracelets for men now.

Or you could always just use a permanent marker and put a cross on your finger or hand. When I first started this, I would realize sometime throughout the day that I hadn't really even thought of, God. What happened to my thinking I prayed to God all the time? I realized I didn't. I was convicted, and I bet you will be too! You'll be amazed how little time you spend with God throughout your day. If this seems silly, just give it a try.

Beth Moore wasn't the first with this idea. She passes the credit herself to Isaiah 44:5 (ESV), "This one will say, 'I am the Lord's,' another will call on the name of Jacob, and another will write on his hand, 'The Lord's,' and name himself by the name of Israel." What will it take for you to remember, moment by moment, you are the Lord's?

Another challenge comes from Jesus while He was being tempted in the wilderness. Then Jesus said to him, "Be gone, Satan! For it is written, 'You shall worship the Lord your God and him only shall you serve'" (Matthew 4:10 ESV).

If Jesus did this, shouldn't we? I know people who still walk through their house and say, "Be gone, Satan!" to cleanse their home. We have forgotten—or we just don't know—the instructions in God's Word to help us live with Him daily. And it's just like anything else. When you fall, you get back up and try again. The only difference—and it's a big one—is we have God and His Spirit strengthening us more each time.

Many times I have prayed this verse. I say it when I'm weak and about to get into something I know I shouldn't. Most often it's my overwhelming desire for chips or cookies, but there are times I say it to get rid of thoughts in my mind that aren't from God. Most of the time it works.

There are those times my desire is so strong that I still turn away from God even though He's there and never turns away from me. What are your desires you need to "Be gone, Satan" over? Don't feel silly walking through your life while saying this. Jesus said it first! Always remember, though, it's our weak flesh when we fail. Never

God! He doesn't fail, He doesn't make mistakes, He's never late, and He's never wrong!

Second, we have to surround ourselves with people doing the same. God instructs us to not walk with Him alone, but with Him and others. I went through a period where I thought I could do it alone, this believer's life, just God and me. But I realized from Him the importance of fellowship with other believers, sharing with and encouraging each other (Matthew 21:12–13; 2 Corinthians 1:3–12, and so many more).

"And let us consider how to stir up one another to love and good works, not neglecting to meet together, as is the habit of some, but encouraging one another, and all the more as you see the Day drawing near" (Hebrews 10:24–25 ESV).

It's an awesome, freeing, contented way of life, being with God always. We are all continually growing and learning. We all have failed and feared in some way or another. And we all know how we need to improve.

Third and last, we have to be honest with ourselves. God already knows—and you might be surprised to find out—who around you sees whether or not you're being honest. They might be praying for you. That's one reason God instructs us to have fellowship (Matthew 18:15–17). I hope and pray you find peace with God, especially if you've never found fault with yourself.

Everything you have gone through—and will go through—has a reason and a purpose. You can let it consume you in a negative way, or you can learn joyously from it in a positive way. Let God guide you to the positive, joyous lifestyle you were created for and know that you will be completed in for eternity.

What are your goals in changing your prayer lifestyle now? Be committed!

_____

_____

_____

_____

_____

_____

_____

_____

_____

_____

"Therefore confess your sins to each other and pray for each other so that you may be healed. The prayer of a righteous person is powerful and effective" (James 5:16 NIV).

"Peace I leave with you, my peace I give unto you: not as the world giveth, give I unto you. Let not your heart be troubled, neither let it be afraid" (John 14:27 KJV).

The Conclusion

A. W. Tozer, pastor, author, and editor, said and is quoted in his book, *The Quotable Tozer*, "It is possible to worship God with our lips and not worship God with our lives. But I want to tell you that if your life doesn't worship God, your lips don't worship God either."

None of us worships God like we could and should. All of us are looking for something. Remember from the introduction that we need to realize we're not searching for answers but seeking the answer that is already there. Do you think Eve was searching and seeking answers when she ate of the apple? Did she eat the apple for God's glory or her own?

She ate the apple so she could know all that God knew. It would bring about the benefit of all though because we would, through this sinful fall, all need God to send a Savior if we only believe. From this one act of God's gracious and forgiving love, we would have the privilege to know Him through His Son, Jesus our Savior (Genesis 3; Romans 3:23; John 3:16).

If you're a believer, God is already transforming your heart, and the Holy Spirit is residing there. For those people who are not believers, Satan lives in their hearts. They have all of Satan's emotions, hate, envy, bitterness, and more. Their thoughts are not of love and good but of violence and revenge. And these are some of the best of people.

This is why we need to pray for the lost fervently. We pray for our loved ones, our sisters and brothers in Christ. We pray for their needs and healing, but we need to pray for the lost for the same reasons but mostly for salvation, not only for their own good but for ours.

I didn't know this as a child. I didn't pray for the people who were so cruel to me. I remember praying, "Be with Grandma and Grandpa," those kind of childhood prayers, but I also remember praying for a safe, secure home again. What I mostly remember praying after my mother's death were actually pleas to God, "Why? Why am I going through this? Why did Mama die?"

I now know those were the kind of prayers God wanted to hear, my innermost desires and feelings, my hurts and pain, for myself. And maybe in a way, I was including the lost around me because I did pray, "Why are they doing these things?" and "Make the meanness stop, God." I also prayed for a safe, secure, loving home again. This prayer wasn't answered until I was grown with my own children, but it was answered.

And God is so faithful. I even understand the "whys" that I prayed. I know why everything happened the way it did. Why? So I could share and tell my experiences and thoughts about life, suffering, and the love of God that healed me so much that I could write it all down for unbelieving people and you. I am forever thankful to God for everything.

This life is not about you. It's not about me. It's really about our families and friends and all of those who are nonbelievers. It's about investing toward your eternity and theirs. Share with them the true King and His kingdom, Jesus, the everlasting gift. This world is broken. It was broken from Adan and Eve, and we carry on the brokenness, but we can help to change that. We have the power of our testimony. We can pass on our account and give our witness of what Jesus has done for us. Start by and never stop praying.

Read God's Word. Read the verses, and read them again and again. Read them in order, out of order, and together. Listen to what God is saying through them.

Know what God expects. Being a believer is easy. God has already made the decisions for you. You only have to read and know them. If there were no expectations, it'd be like a very wealthy man giving his children extremely large trust funds and telling them to do whatever they wished.

How would they live without expectations? Would they live good, wholesome lives, or would their tendency be to do all the wrong things? It is the same with us, once we believe. We've been given an extremely large trust fund, but unlike the wealthy man's children, we have been given expectations and instructions to guide us to use it wisely, from our heavenly Father, God.

Ask. "Therefore I say to you, all things for which you pray and ask, believe that you have received them, and they shall be granted you" (Mark 11:24 NASB).

Do. "I will tell of your name to my brothers; in the midst of the congregation I will praise you" (Psalm 22:22 ESV). We are like Paul in Philippians 1:12. Our story, whatever we have gone through, serves to further the gospel of Jesus, but we have to share. We have to tell our story of Jesus's salvation to others (Hebrews 13:16). We need to be a living sacrifice (Romans 12:1–2). We need to give from what we have (Philippians 4:14–18). And we need to continually praise God (Hebrews 13:15). When we don't, we have cheated God (Malachi 1:14), and our worship is not worship.

How do these questions apply in your life now?

Who is God?

_____

_____

_____

_____

_____

_____

_____

_____

_____

Who is Jesus?

_____

_____

_____

_____

_____

_____

_____

Who is the Holy Spirit?

_____

_____

_____

_____

_____

_____

_____

_____

_____

Is our God and you conditional or unconditional?

_____

_____

_____

_____

_____

_____

_____

_____

_____

What is the ultimate reason and purpose for a believer?

_____

_____

_____

_____

_____

_____

_____

_____

How does prayer and the way you pray, together with others, relate to these questions?

_____

_____

_____

_____

_____

_____

_____

_____

_____

How does prayer and the way you pray relate to you?

_____

_____

_____

_____

_____

_____

_____

_____

"Come and hear, all you who fear God, and I will tell what he has done for my soul. I cried to him with my mouth, and high praise was on my tongue. If I had cherished iniquity in my heart, the Lord would not have listened. But truly God has listened; he has attended to the voice of my prayer. Blessed be God, because he has not rejected my prayer or removed his steadfast love from me!" (Psalm 66:16–20 ESV)

"Be anxious for nothing, but in everything by prayer and supplication with thanksgiving let your requests be made known to God. And the peace of God, which surpasses all comprehension, shall guard your hearts and your minds in Christ Jesus" (Philippians 4:6–7 NASB).

I do hope and pray this book has left you feeling encouraged. While we all have things to work on in our lives and our walk with God, He gives us all the guidance and encouragement we need while on this earth! And God promises,

> And there shall be no more curse: but the throne of God and of the Lamb shall be in it; and his servants shall serve him: and they shall see his face; and his name shall be in their foreheads. And there shall be no night there; and they need no candle, neither light of the sun; for the Lord God giveth them light: and they shall reign for ever and ever. (Revelation 22:3–5 KJV)

Thank You, God. Thank You, Jesus. Thank You, Holy Spirit!

Bible Verse Reference

Introduction

1 Timothy 6:12 (NASB); Matthew 6:33 (KJV); Acts 8:29–35 (ESV); 2 Timothy 3:16–17 (ESV); Colossians 3:16–17 (ESV)

Introduction to Section 1: The Trinity

Psalm 25:4–5 (LB); 1 Peter 1:2 (LB)

Chapter 1: Our God

Exodus 3:13–14 (NASB); Psalm 148:13 (NASB); Psalm 83:16–18 (KJV); Psalm 25:14 (KJV); Psalm 25:14 (ESV); 2 Chronicles 16:9 (NASB); Psalms 17, 89, 145; 1 John 4:8; Psalm 145:17–20 (KJV); Psalm 51:5; Psalm 51:14; Job 9:10 (NIV); Job 23:8–12; 2 Corinthians 1:3–5; Psalm 51:15 (ESV); 1 Corinthians 1:10; Matthew 6:10 (KJV); Malachi 3:6 (KJV); 2 Corinthians 4:16–17 (NIV); 1 Corinthians 10:31 (ESV); Psalm 34:8 (ESV)

Chapter 2: Jesus

John 14:6 (NIV); John 2:23–25 (LB); Matthew 1:23; Isaiah 7:14; Luke 1; Isaiah 7:14, 9:6, 11:1–5, 53; Daniel 7:13–14; Zechariah 13:1; Luke 10:21 (LB); John 6:38 (KJV); Matthew 10:32 (RSV); Matthew 26:28 (KJV); Psalm 118:25; Psalm 3; Matthew 21:9; Matthew 26:39; Mark 14:35–36; Luke 22:42; Hebrews 2:17–18; 1 John 4:18–19 (ESV); Philippians 1:29 (NIV); John 20:19–21 (ESV); Philippians 1:27–29; John 3:16–17 (ESV)

Chapter 3: The Holy Spirit (Holy Ghost)

Acts 1, 2; Acts 2:38 (KJV); Romans 6:4–7; Romans 8:26 (LB); John 14:15–17 (GW); Ephesians 1:13–14 (NASB and ESV); Genesis 1:2 (KJV); Romans 14:17–18 (NASB); Galatians 5:16–17 (NASB); Galatians 5:22–23 (NASB); Romans 8:26; Psalm 139:7–10 (NIV); 1 Corinthians 3:8; 2 Corinthians 5:10; Revelations 2:23; Revelation 22:12; Acts 2:3–4 (ESV); Luke 4:1; Isaiah 61:1 (NASB); Luke 1:34–35 (ESV); Acts 1:8 (NIV)

Chapter 4: The Trinity

John 14:26 (ESV); Jude 20–23 (ESV); Revelation 19:7–9; Ephesians 3; Joel 2:27–29, 32 (ML); Isaiah 54:5; Revelation 19:7–9; John 15:26–27 (LB); 2 Corinthians 13:14 (ESV)

Introduction to Section 2: Expectations

John 14:22–23 (ESV); Matthew 4:17 (KJV); Matthew 4:19 (KJV); Mark 4:1–10 (ESV); Ephesians 4:22–24 (RSV); Philippians 1:21 (NASB); 1 Kings 19:7–14 (LB); 1 Kings 19:15–18; Psalm 46:10

Chapter 5: God's Conditions and Unconditional Love

Ephesians 2:8–9; Acts 11:26, 26:28; 1 Peter 4:16; Revelation 3:15-16 (ESV); Deuteronomy 8:14; 2 Chronicles 20:33; Proverbs 1:32; Luke 12:18–21; Revelation 3:16; Genesis 1:22; Genesis 1:28; Genesis 6:9 (KJV); Genesis 6:9 (ESV); Genesis 17:1 (KJV); Genesis 17:1 (ESV); Psalm 51:5 (KJV); Psalm 51:5 (NIV); Psalm 119:105; Proverbs 7:2–3; Matthew 4:4; Romans 15:4; Ephesians 6:17; Hebrews 4:12; 2 Timothy 3:16–17; 1 Corinthians 13; 1 Corinthians 3:16 (RS); Psalm 139:14 (NASB)

Chapter 6: Our Conditions and Unconditional Love

Acts 26:15–20; Psalm 119:57–60 (NIV); Hebrews 4:16 (NIV); Luke 23:34 (KJV); Deuteronomy 11:18–19 (NASB); John 3:16; John 13:35;

John 14:21, 17:23; 1 Corinthians 3:16; 1 John 4:8; Jeremiah 31:3 (ESV); Mark 7:20–23 (ESV)

Chapter 7: Our Life as a Believer

Matthew 9:9; Matthew 8:22; Joshua 1:9; Psalm 139:7–12; Isaiah 43:2; Zephaniah 3:17; 1 Thessalonian 5:15–18 (KJV); Luke 6:31; James 3:13–18 (NASB); Galatians 5:19–21; Luke 6:23; Matthew 5:16; Matthew 5:13; 1 Peter 1:13–16 (NASB); Joel 1:3 (ESV); Isaiah 6:8; 1 Samuel 3:10; Jude; James 3:14; Isaiah 43:18–20; Philippians 3:13–14; Revelation 21:5 (NIV); Matthew 28:19; Acts 2:47 (ESV)

Introduction to Section 3: The Pursuit of Prayer

Psalm 5; Exodus 28:36, 39:30; Luke 7:36–50; Luke 7:50 (NIV); 1 Thessalonians 5:16–18 (ESV)

Chapter 8: Past Prayers

Genesis 3:8–13, 4:9; Genesis 4:25–26 (KJV); James 5:15; Acts 2:42; Philippians 4:6; Psalm 95:2–6; Matthew 26:39; 1 Timothy 2:1; Psalm 51; Jude 20 (NASB); Psalm 5:3 (NIV); 2 Samuel 7:18; Mark 11:25; 2 Chronicles 6:13; Daniel 6:10; Luke 22:41; Ephesians 3:14; Matthew 26:39; Mark 14:35; 1 Timothy 2:8; Matthew 6:6–13 (NIV); Matthew 6:6–7 (NASB); Job 42, 42:5; Philippians 4:6–7; 1 Chronicles 4:9–10 (NIV)

Chapter 9: Present Prayers

Psalm 66:18 (ESV); James 5:13–16; Matthew 21:21–22 (NASB); Exodus 8:12–13 (NASB); Joshua 9:14 (ESV); Joshua 10:12–14; 1 Thessalonians 5: 16 (NASB); Jeremiah 17:7–8 (NIV)

Chapter 10: Future Prayers and Your Prayer Lifestyle

James 4:2 (NIV); James 5:16; Isaiah 44:5 (ESV); Matthew 4:10 (ESV); Matthew 21:12–13; 2 Corinthians 1:3–12; Hebrews 10:24–25 (ESV); Matthew 18:15–17; James 5:16 (NIV); John 14:27 (KJV)

The Conclusion

Genesis 3; Romans 3:23; John 3:16; Mark 11:24 (NASB); Psalm 22:22 (ESV); Philippians 1:12; Hebrews 13:16; Romans 12:1–2; Philippians 4:14–18; Hebrews 13:15; Malachi 1:14; Psalm 66:16–20 (ESV); Philippians 4:6–7 (NASB); Revelation 22:3–5 (KJV)

References

Smith, William. *Smith's Bible Dictionary*. Philadelphia: A.J. Holman Company.

Webster's New World Pocket Dictionary. Foster City: IDG, 2000.

Wikipedia

God's Word to the Nations. *God's Word Translation*. 1995.

Dictionary.com

Carter, Joe. *9 Things You Should Know about Prayer in the Bible*.

Lockyer, Herbert. *All the Prayers of the Bible*.

Tozer, A.W. *The Quotable Tozer: A Topical Compilation of the Wisdom and Insight of A.W. Tozer*. Baker Books, 2018.

About the Author

Lisa Lynn is a wife, mother, and grandma. She spent her childhood in a religious home until her mom was murdered, leaving her vulnerable and thrown into a new, evil world. She would then grow up seeking, searching, and studying the foundation her mother told her about, the saving grace of God through His Son, Jesus. She has written and led numerous Bible studies, classes, and public devotions for children, teens, adults, and elderly people and never misses an opportunity to speak about what God does in our lives. After years of secrets and silence, she tells everything in her book, *Unraveled, Time to Tell,* and now guides you in *Unraveled, Time to Hear: An Investment toward Your Eternity.*

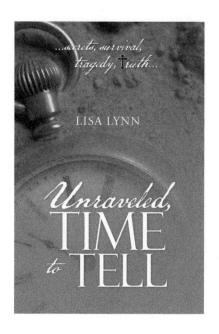

Unraveled, Time to Tell

When we write a book as I wrote this one, we write of what we know or feel firsthand. It's something we want to share. I was shown something that helped me so much through the hardest, darkest situations a person can endure. I didn't want what came into my life as a little girl. I didn't ask for it or understand it, but there was nothing I could do but learn how to survive, which I did. Survival only came with the help from the only one who can really give us help in those kinds of horrible, confusing, and self-destructive events. That only one is God! This book is really about Him, His examples, and His words with my experiences. It is a true story of the unending grace and encouragement of God.

"Unraveled, Time to Tell" Chapters Categorized for Further Reference

Chapter 1: The Darkest Day—Murder

Chapter 2: The First Nine Years—Memories

Chapter 3: My New Normal—Change, Abuse

Chapter 4: First Stepfamily—Abuse, Revenge

Chapter 5: Always with a Smile—Afflictions, Salvation

Chapter 6: Second Stepfamily—More Change, More Abuse

Chapter 7: My Brother—Suicide and Salvation

Chapter 8: Life away from the Next Two—God's Plan Continues through Trials

Chapter 9: Growing Up in Christ—Fear and Understanding

Chapter 10: Marriage and Beyond—Pregnancy, Abortion, Marriage, and Parenting

Chapter 11: Raising Children While God's Raising Me—Parenting, Obedience

Chapter 12: Marriage and Beyond Continues—Marriage, More Revelations